Your Child's Career in Music and Entertainment

The Prudent Parent's Guide from Start to Stardom

Steven C. Beer

with

Kathryne Badura

ALLWORTH PRESS
NEW YORK

Allworth Press books may be purchased in bulk at special discounts for sales promotion, corporate gifts, fund-raising, or educational purposes. Special editions can also be created to specifications. For details, contact the Special Sales Department, Allworth Press, 307 West 36th Street, 11th Floor, New York, NY 10018 or info@skyhorsepublishing.com.

19 18 17 16 15   5 4 3 2 1

Published by Allworth Press, an imprint of Skyhorse Publishing, Inc. 307 West 36th Street, 11th Floor, New York, NY 10018.

Allworth Press® is a registered trademark of Skyhorse Publishing, Inc.®, a Delaware corporation.

www.allworth.com

Cover design by Mary Belibasakis

Library of Congress Cataloging-in-Publication Data is available on file.

Print ISBN: 978-1-62153-480-8

Ebook ISBN: 978-1-62153-490-7

Printed in the United States of America.

More Praise for *Your Child's Career in Music and Entertainment*

"I cannot imagine a more useful text for parents trying to get a leg up for their children in the entertainment industry. Steven's advice is invaluable."—Rebecca Lambrecht, music manager and founder of the Chicane Group

"Steven Beer is a knowledgeable, experienced counselor who understands the challenges and opportunities facing families who aspire to success in the entertainment industry. I can't think of a better authority to tackle this subject."—Cliff Chenfeld, co-CEO, Razor & Tie Music and Kidz Bop

"Steven Beer is an entertainment lawyer, industry consultant, and parent in the entertainment industry who has successfully guided many young people on the complex journey to a career in music and entertainment. If your child is serious about a career in the "business," this book is a must-have. Accessible and filled with insider information, resources, case studies, and legal advice, it is invaluable!"—Michael Rapaport, actor

"Steven Beer has written a lucid, sweepingly comprehensive yet straightforward guide both practical and inspiring for all parents lucky enough to have talented children to nurture into a career in entertainment."—James Toback, filmmaker

"I was floored by the thorough understanding Steven Beer has been able to achieve. He leaves no stone left unturned in explaining the pitfalls and questions every parent with a talented child has. It should be the "turn-to Bible" for all families in the business. I could not recommend it more highly."—Ron Schaefer, director of French Woods Festival of the Performing Arts

"This book is a roadmap from a highly experienced, knowledgeable guide for any parent whose child wants (begs) to pursue a career in the music or entertainment business. It provides advice on each step of the journey and offers practical steps and tactics to ensure the best possibility for success."—Susan Solovay, professional parent

Table of Contents

Foreword

By Larry Rudolph

IF I HAVE LEARNED ANYTHING from my years of experience in the entertainment industry, it is that navigating your way through it is like trying to navigate a vast, uncharted wilderness. Without a guide, it is impossible to find your way through.

At the start of our careers, in 1993, Steven and I founded the law firm of Rudolph & Beer, LLP. Our practice focused on entertainment law, and much of our time was devoted to the legal protection and representation of emerging young artists. We didn't stop there, however. Steven and I also took on the role of handling many of the bigger-picture management issues that arose for our rising star clients. We realized that we were the "guides" these young entertainers needed. With the right management, career development, and counseling, we helped our clients achieve their show business dreams and grow into worldwide phenomena, such as the Backstreet Boys, *NSYNC, Aaron Carter, and Lady Gaga.

During our time at Rudolph & Beer, we had met Britney Spears and her family when she was just thirteen years old. Steven and I had the unique experience of representing her at this early point in her career and developed and guided her to the point when she first signed with Jive Records in 1999 and released her debut album, *Baby One More Time*. We managed her throughout the early stages of her teenage career and watched her grow from a sweet Louisiana girl to an international superstar. Although I have left the practice of law to serve as Britney's full-time manager and have been by her side for most of her career, Steven still actively practices entertainment law in New York City.

When Steven told me he was writing this guide, I was excited. An important lesson we learned from our years of managing and representing young stars was that every successful child had a grounded, thoughtful, and involved support system: their parents. Without such support and a firm parental hand, any success was short-lived. I often get questions from parents in the industry about aspects of their child's career and how to handle them but am unable to properly answer them all.

This book is a great tool for parents looking for that guidance in handling or even just starting their child's career, and there is no one better to learn from than Steven Beer. Not only is Steven experienced with high-profile entertainment transactions involving young artists, but he also brings to his work a unique management perspective that most, if not all, other attorneys lack. In his over twenty-five years of practicing law and managing artists, Steven has established many important entertainment industry relationships with various casting directors, agents, producers, directors, and other managers. He and these industry insiders have a great deal of wisdom to impart upon parents and their children who are considering careers in the music and entertainment industry, and this book lays it all out for them in a way that is straightforward and easy to understand. As an added bonus, having been blessed with three talented boys who themselves have dabbled in the entertainment industry, Steven too has been in your shoes as a prudent parent of a child in show business. Having taken on the role himself, he empathizes with your frustrations and concerns and knows what it is that you need to know. I cannot think of anyone more qualified than Steven to guide you and your family through the difficult but rewarding journey of launching your child's career and wish you all the best of luck!

Author's Note

I REMEMBER THE CALL LIKE it was yesterday. I was sitting in my law office preparing some agreements for a new film production. "He got the part," my wife, Bonnie, enthusiastically reported. My thirteen-year-old son, Max, loved theater. He studied acting at school and camp and participated in community theater groups where we live in New York City. In his spare time, Max occasionally auditioned for roles in professional productions. We thought it was merely a constructive after-school activity, so we were stunned to learn that a major regional theater company actually cast him in a lead role for a touring production of Neil Simon's *Lost in Yonkers*. My wife's initial excitement quickly turned to reticence. Her voiced lowered when she asked me, "What should we do?" Unprepared for this question, I responded that I did not know.

Although I had gained considerable experience as a media and entertainment attorney, manager, and consultant guiding young artists and their families about the music and entertainment business, my compass lost its bearing the minute I tried to apply my experience to my son's career. My deep personal connection to my child disabled me from seeing matters through an objective lens.

I soon realized that my vision was blurred by a set of complicated factors. Bonnie and I understood that, for Max, landing the lead role in a prominent production was his dream come true. We knew a part like this would immerse him into a world and culture that made him happy. Reality set in, however, when the production company advised us matter-of-factly that this role required a six- to eight-month commitment. Max would have to leave his school to travel to Ohio, Florida, and New Jersey for his performances. Although they would provide him with a tutor, we would need to provide adult supervision.

Bonnie and I were overwhelmed and deeply conflicted. We both had full-time jobs and two other sons (Alex and Gabriel) with diverse interests and activities. We were not in a position to disregard our employment and family obligations. At the same time, we did not want to pull the rug out from under Max and deny him this dream opportunity. We desperately needed to figure this out but were clueless about the particular logistics of this substantial commitment. What should we do?

Answering this question proved more challenging than anticipated, mostly because we did not have a road map to help us figure out a responsible path. My role as an industry professional did not fully prepare me to grasp all of the questions we needed to address. Bonnie and I realized that there were no handy resources to which we could refer to help us understand the complete breadth and scope of this opportunity.

Once the dust settled, we began to assess the challenges involved and sacrifices to be made. We brainstormed, soul searched, and ultimately decided to figure out a way to make this work for Max. Toward this end, we reached out to Max's brothers, our parents (who unselfishly volunteered to accompany him), and Max's educators and engaged them in our problem-solving quest. With a considerable degree of trepidation, we decided to take a leap of faith and agreed to support Max in this once-in-a-lifetime opportunity.

Our family dilemma, sparked by Max's professional opportunity, served as a catalyst to this book. My search for reliable, practical, and contemporary reference materials gave me the incentive to prepare a prudent parents' guide for those considering similar situations. I hope this book provides you with a useful resource as you encounter the joys, perils, and sacrifices associated with your child's career in music and entertainment.

Acknowledgments

WRITING YOUR CHILD'S CAREER IN *Music and Entertainment: The Prudent Parent's Guide* has been a rewarding adventure, and I have many to thank for their help and support along the way.

My greatest appreciation is for my amazing wife, Bonnie, and my three wonderful sons, Alex, Max and Gabe, all of whom encouraged me to write this book. My dad passed away several years ago. He and my mother, Ronni, dropped everything to accompany Max on the road when he toured with the Papermill Playhouse co-production of Neil Simon's *Lost in Yonkers*. I dedicate this book to them. I am particularly grateful for the contributions of Kathryne Badura, Larry Rudolph, Rebecca Lambrecht, Lindsay Donn Mann, Andrew Bauer, and Ron Schaeffer, without whom this book could not have been written.

Many thanks also to Lisbeth Bartlett, Jon Batiste, Isaac Baumfeld, Jeffrey Beer, Larry Beer, Michael Beer, Eric Brown, Aaron Carter, Bob Carter, Jane Carter, Cliff Chenfeld, Cari Cole, DeeDee DeBartlo, Eileen DeNobile, Stephen Dubner, Lew Eisenberg, Nancy Farrell, Andrea Flink, Ken Feinberg, Trapper Felides, Tess Filsoof, Arlette Goldstein, Kenneth Goldstein, Nick Gordon, Emily Grace, Geoffrey Gray, Susan Jones, Ilyana Kadushin, Jill Kargman, Keith Kelly, Susan Konig, Barry Klarberg, Janice Kubow, Lady Gaga, Dr. Jon LaPook, Elizabeth Landes, William Landes, Jimmy Landry, Kate Lear, John Germain Leto, Halle Madia, Reed Martin, Guy Mastrion, Kathryn Maughan, Jonathan McHugh, Beth Melsky, Maria Miles, Lara Jill Miller, Binta Naimbi-Brown, Julie Nunes, Scott Osman, Marc Pellegrino, Si Si Penaloza, Jonathan Platt, Michael Rapaport, Jon Reiss, Neil Rosini, Michael Rudell, Jillian Sanders, Sariah, Ann Sarnoff, Richard Sarnoff, Susan Shaffer Solovay, Britney Spears, Adrienne Stern, Gary Su, Taylor Swift, Harvey Tanton, Brian Thomas, James Toback, Steven Tyler,

Adam Unze, Greg Uzelac, John Wager, Errol Wander, Jason Ward, Ken Weinrib, and Zoe Wright.

—Steven C. Beer

I would like to thank Steven for his years of guidance and affording me the opportunity to work with him on this exciting and groundbreaking book. I also thank Lindsay Donn Mann for her contributions and friendship. I send warm and loving thoughts to all of my family, friends, and loved ones for their support and encouragement, in particular, my parents, brother, and Babci—who has always served as my greatest example of strength and determination. Finally, I thank Ms. Marilyn Rich for instilling in me my love of the written word and teaching me that "you are who you are when nobody else is looking."

—Kathryne Badura

Introduction

How Do You and Your Child Define "Success"?

WE ARE LIVING IN A New Renaissance[1]. In many respects, there has never been a better time for your child to pursue a career in music and entertainment. Largely due to developments in digital technology, the costs to create content (music recordings, music videos, independent films, etc.) have declined dramatically over the past decade. At the same time, and for similar reasons, access to the marketplace has never been easier. We regularly read and hear about numerous young artists like Justin Bieber who established a following on digital platforms such as YouTube and from there were able to launch a global, high-profile career.

The emerging digital entertainment universe has become a new place for recognition and discovery. Talent agencies, management and production companies, and record labels all track online content and trends in search of the next big thing. Like the GPS system in your car indicates, there is more than one route to arrive at your destination—your child's success. As you embark on this journey, be mindful of potential opportunities to be explored down emerging new avenues.

There is no single definition of "success." In the New Renaissance, the artist can define success subjectively on his or her own terms. He or she can pursue a career that is personally meaningful and satisfying, regardless of the financial rewards or industry-established benchmarks such as a Grammy Award, a Tony, or an Oscar. "Success" today is not uniform but comes in many shapes and sizes, so it is essential to carefully consider what success means to your child and to develop an appropriate success plan to achieve it.

How do you and your child define success? Take your time exploring this critical question. Once you and your child subjectively determine what "success" looks like, you can begin to chart a customized route to this unique destination. Your definition of success will shape virtually every decision you will encounter along the way, including your budget, timetable, representatives, where you live, and how and where your child will be educated.

Listen carefully to your child, and you will learn how to steer the career car in the right direction. A child's perspective can surprise you, too. I learned this lesson when my oldest child, Alex, declined to explore professional opportunities after his high school band won a national competition. He and his bandmates loved playing together and did not want anything to interfere with their experience. For my son and his bandmates, success meant recording their music and performing it on stage before their friends and fans.

From my personal family experience, I learned that not all currency is green. It turns out that the greatest reward is not always money but the rich experience gained through your child's creative pursuits. The prudent parent appreciates the value of the journey. The time spent on this trek will bond you with your child and teach him or her important lessons about life and the pursuit of creative fulfillment.

Enjoy the ride.

Go Look in a Mirror

Think of your child's career in entertainment as a car. No matter how talented, your child lacks sufficient judgment to responsibly drive the car alone on the road to success. He or she must therefore be securely fastened in the passenger seat, while you take the wheel. By following the road map you create, you will help your child achieve success by navigating the career car in a diligent direction. Mindful of the potential hazards on the prospective journey, it is your job to fasten your seatbelt, firmly grasp the steering wheel with both hands, and adeptly navigate the career car on the sometimes-treacherous path to your destination.

As the prudent parent, you must maintain a laser-like focus with both eyes on the road. You will be tempted by human nature and industry forces to speed the car past certain road signs. Putting the pedal to the metal, however, can be perilous. There are numerous obstacles, many of which are difficult to anticipate. Should the career car go off the road for any reason, only you will be to blame. It is therefore crucial to be well-prepared for the journey you are about to take with your child.

Looking at yourself in a mirror encourages you, the prudent parent, to follow one of the key rules of driving: check and adjust your mirrors. Before any car trip, it is wise to make sure your view from behind the wheel is focused and unobstructed. This precaution gives you a handle on surrounding circumstances, allowing you to drive safely to your destination. Likewise, you, as the diligent conductor on your child's journey to success, must ensure that you have a clear view of the path you will follow, as well as an understanding of the responsibilities and other circumstances that a career in entertainment entails. How informed are you about the music and entertainment industry? Have you recruited experts to help guide you in areas in which you are not experienced? Have you defined "success" and created a customized business plan and budget? Do you know your state's requirements with respect to its labor laws and the financial aspects of your child's business engagements? Understanding these questions before you start will allow you to safely and cautiously navigate your child's career to the ultimate destination: show business success.

The mirror also reflects the significant role *you* play in this whole process. It forces you to come face-to-face with the reality of the circumstances surrounding the decision to embark on this journey. Regarding yourself in the mirror, you, the prudent parent, must come to terms with your child's objectives and motivations. How badly does your child desire a career? What is he or she willing to sacrifice? Do these concessions make sense to you? How invested are you in your child's career? What are you willing to sacrifice? Are you willing and able to finance your child's career? Are you willing to reduce your active personal involvement with your household responsibilities, your other children, and your marriage? It is OK if you are unable to answer these questions right away. Take your time to consider these questions honestly. A mirror never lies.

Once you have meaningfully examined yourself, tilt the mirror toward your child so that he or she, too, can thoughtfully explore and understand his or her motivations in pursuing a show business career. Have your child consider what he or she is willing to do and willing to give up. Ask him or her to explain, "Why do you want to go into show business? Is it because you love performing? Is it because you want to look 'cool' to your friends or seek our (your parents') approval? Are you willing to put in a lot of time and effort and give up many of your other hobbies, interests, and free time to do it?" By making your child seriously think about and articulate the answers to these questions, you can better gauge whether your child is fully prepared and properly motivated to make this commitment.

These are but a few of the critical questions discussed within these pages. This book seeks to make you aware of both potential hazards and opportunities within the entertainment industry and keep you and your child from getting lost along the way. You may not be able to answer all of these questions during your initial self-examination. After reading this book, go back and ask yourselves those questions again. Hopefully, the lessons presented here will help clarify any uncertainties or reservations you may have and enable you, the prudent parent, to help your child reach his or her destination—a successful and constructive career.

CHAPTER 1

Packing for the Trip

I think my child has talent. How do I know if he or she can make it in the world of music and entertainment?

LET'S FACE IT: MANY PARENTS believe their children to be extraordinary. They proudly extol their achievements and abilities at every given opportunity, sometimes embellishing to make their child seem even more impressive. Though this approach may work in everyday social circles and can build your child's self-esteem, such "puffing" will not provide children with any benefit when trying to make it in the music and entertainment industry. In fact, it may actually put them at a disadvantage by building up false hopes for children who honestly do not have what it takes to compete at an industry level. Pursuing an entertainment career for your child, when based upon a biased view of your child's talents, is unlikely to yield success and may cause you to incur unnecessary expenses and set your child up for disappointment. Therefore, I encourage you to take off your rose-colored "parent glasses" and assess your child's talent and character from an objective point of view.

Ask Yourself

First and foremost, you must ask yourself, "Does my child have talent?" Though your child may be "good" at something, be it singing, dancing, acting, or playing an instrument, he or she may not be "good enough" for a successful career in show business. This evaluation may seem harsh, but a certain caliber of talent is necessary to compete at a professional level in the entertainment industry. The higher up in the industry your child seeks to go, the more competitive the talent. Just because a child has participated in performance activities such as school plays or choirs does not mean that he or she will necessarily succeed in landing a record deal or a role on Broadway. Furthermore, a child who has been repeatedly unsuccessful in being assigned solos in the school concert or getting the lead role in a play at the community theater will probably not succeed at a higher level and is not suited for a career in music and entertainment.

There are certain signs you, as a parent, can look for to determine whether your child has the appropriate level of talent. When people outside the family make it a point to pay unsolicited compliments to you about your child's abilities, it may be an indication that your child does, in fact, have significant talent from an objective standpoint. For example, when an acting or vocal coach, or even just a stranger in the audience, approaches you after your child has sung a solo in a school concert and tells you how wonderful she was, praising her voice and stage presence, it signals that others recognize that your child has extraordinary abilities.

Ask the Professionals

Another way of assessing your child's talent level is to solicit the opinion of seasoned professionals within the music and entertainment industry. Talent agents, managers, producers, directors, and casting agents, to name a few, can offer the best opinions. Not only do they know what level of talent is necessary for a successful career, but they have nothing to gain from making false promises, since they only make money when the child finds success. Manager Eileen DeNobile shares that a manager knows within two minutes whether or not your child has what it takes, and although it can be very uncomfortable to have to pass on a child, it is a necessary part of her job. Her simple answer to parents who are invited to meet with her and ask whether their child has what it takes for a successful career is, "You wouldn't be sitting here if your child *didn't* have what it takes." Halle Madia, a former agent specializing in young talent development at Innovative Artists Agency, elaborates on the qualities agents use to identify successful child actors. According to Halle, these qualities include personality, genuine interest, and the ability to act naturally. If your child possesses all of these traits, he or she may, in fact, be show business material.

It would also be advisable to seek out the opinion of more than one professional, since they will not always agree, and reach a conclusion based on a consensus of the evaluations. Beware, however, of Svengali-like managers and promoters who hype your child's "star" prospects but ask you to spend thousands of dollars upfront without a track record or reasonable game plan. If their promises sound too good to be true, they probably are.

What It Takes

Though talent is crucial, it is not, in itself, enough to ensure success. As touched upon above, your child's personality is a distinct indication of whether he or she is suited for a career in the music and entertainment industry. Once you have concluded that your child has the talent, you must determine whether his or her demeanor exhibits the characteristics of an entertainer. Show business is not just about a child's presence on stage or on screen when performing. It is about his or her ability to connect with an audience in other contexts and interact with other professionals he or she works with along the way. In his book *Launching Your Child in Show Biz: A Complete Step-By-Step Guide,* Dick Van Patten, a former Broadway child star turned entertainment industry professional, notes that,

> In most cases, what agents look for isn't the traditional kind of talent at all. It's a knack for coming across relaxed and natural. For expressing oneself honestly. For listening and interacting with others. For showing enthusiasm and a willingness to work hard. For caring about doing the best job possible. Without all that, even the most gifted prodigy in the world will be in for a tough time in the job market.[2]

It is therefore important that your child be relatively outgoing and confident. It is a good sign if he or she loves attention. He or she should be comfortable with strangers, since a career in music and entertainment involves meeting and working with new people on a daily basis. Your child should also have no problems answering questions and conversing in an unfamiliar setting. Shyness will be a detriment to his or her career since confidence not only makes a performance more enjoyable to others but creates an air of amiability and pleasantry that will increase popularity and encourage more professionals to want to work with your child. Furthermore, a pleasant and outgoing personality will cause more people in the public to find your child "likeable" and easy to relate to, thus increasing his or her appeal.

Just because your child runs around the house, singing or putting on shows for you and your family and friends does not mean he or she is ready to perform professionally. Though your child can showcase his or her talent in front of people he or she is comfortable around, it is a completely different experience to perform in front of strangers. He or she must be able to perform, at any time, in front of agents, directors, producers, and other professionals without falling subject to shyness or stage fright. An agent meets with dozens of children a day and has neither the time nor the patience to wait for your child to "warm up" to him.

Furthermore, a child must exhibit a certain degree of independence from his or her parents since they will not always be able to stand by holding his or her hand. A child who needs his or her parent present at all times in order to feel comfortable will not fare well when, during a performance, the parent must stay off to the side and out of sight.

Though an outgoing and confident personality is necessary, so is an ability to listen and take direction. There will be many people working with your child who will require a certain degree of maturity and cooperation in order to help your child establish his or her career. For example, if a record producer envisions a certain sound for a song, your child must be able to listen to his direction and adapt his or her style in order to produce the desired result. Agents, managers, instructors, and other members of your child's "career team" will continue to shape and mold your child's sound and image throughout his or her career. Your child must be willing to follow their lead.

Finally, a child must show resilience and an ability to deal with rejection. The music and entertainment industry can be a world full of disappointments. Your child will undoubtedly go on hundreds of auditions and in turn receive hundreds of rejections. It is important for him or her to not be easily discouraged and to immediately pick him- or herself right back up and get back in the game. Sensitivity and tears are expected in the face of rejection, but if your child is taken to easily admitting defeat or abandoning a goal, he or she will not survive in the ultra-competitive world of music and entertainment. Persistence in this field is crucial. Success does not come easily, and your child must be able to deal with the probable failures that come before it.

Determining whether your child "has what it takes" to have a successful career in the music and entertainment industry is perhaps the most difficult part of getting started. It requires brutal honesty and an objective outlook that is often hard for parents to undertake. Going through this honest assessment, however, will not only save you and your child much disappointment in the future if he or she is not meant for this field, it will also provide confidence and motivation in continuing the journey if your child does, in fact, have the ability to compete for a career in the music and entertainment world.

How do I know my child is serious about a career in music and entertainment or if it's just a passing whim?

Initiative and Enthusiasm

The key factor in determining whether your child really wants a career in music and entertainment is "self-motivation." Perhaps the biggest mistake that even the most prudent of parents make is getting their child into the field because *they* want him or her to have a career in entertainment. This is a recipe for disaster. Although sometimes a child may happen to want a career as much as his or her parent does in these situations, a child may feel forced to perform and become angered by, and possibly even resentful of, his or her parent's self-serving manipulation. Such situations often result in the stereotypical nightmare of "stage parents." Furthermore, the child may not put forth his or her best efforts, wasting the time and resources of both parent and child. Van Patten, a child-to-adult actor success, tells parents that, "It's not enough for *you* to want your child to succeed as a performer." Your child must want it as much, if not more: *He's* the one who's going to have to take those lessons and give those readings; *she's* the one who will need to invest a great deal of free time today to achieve a show business career tomorrow."[3] A showing of support or gentle encouragement is key in developing your child's career, but pushing will reduce any enjoyment from the experience. The best way to prevent this common mistake is by being honest with yourself. Ask yourself, as a parent, "Am I just encouraging my child to pursue a career in music and entertainment because I want my child to be famous or want to live vicariously through them, or has my child actually shown a desire for a career in this industry?" Again, complete self-honesty is necessary when answering this question. If you are either unsure of your answer or find that you are more interested in a career for your child than your child is, you, the prudent parent that you are, may want to reconsider getting your child into show business.

Signs of self-motivation are fairly obvious. A motivated child will most likely come right out and make his or her parents expressly aware of an interest in a career in music and entertainment. He will hear a child like himself on the radio or see him on television and exclaim, "I can do that! I want to do that." The prudent parent must be wary of such expressions, however, and ensure that they are frequent and sustained, not simply an occasional passing thought. In addition, a motivated child will make independent efforts to make it known that he or she has a strong interest in performing. For example, if your child auditions for school plays and performs in talent shows on his or her own, this is an indication that your child is prepared to take performing seriously. Such activities entail much time and energy, and your child's voluntary participation signals that he or she may be willing to invest the effort into developing and showcasing his or her musical or theatrical talent required of a career in music and entertainment. Beth Melsky, a casting director with thirty years of experience casting young actors, reaffirms that before talent is even evaluated, the child needs to want to be in the audition room in the first place. When drive meets talent, a successful career in entertainment is possible. In the course of practicing entertainment law and counseling artists for over twenty-five years, I have become quite familiar with the qualities of a child performer destined for stardom. Upon first meeting young performer Stefani Germanotta, I instantly recognized the unique combination of talent and character in the sixteen-year-old who would someday become the world-renowned Lady Gaga. My conversation with Joe Germanotta, Stefani's father, contributed to my confidence in my belief that she could someday be a force in the business. It is worth noting that, while Joe accompanied Stefani during the initial meetings, he always maintained a supportive and professional presence.

It can also be helpful to simply observe your child at play or during "down time" to determine if he or she has the necessary motivation. If your child engages in music- and performance-related activities during times in which he or she can be doing anything he or she pleases, and becomes so involved in doing so that he or she seems to lose all concept of time, it is clear that therein lies a substantial interest and enjoyment in performance. Some telltale signs of this love of performing include performing in talent shows, listening nonstop to the Broadway station in digital radio, putting on shows with friends, walking around the house singing, or forming a garage band. Because your child sees performing and music and entertainment as "fun," he or she will be more likely to continue to view it as such while pursuing it as a career. As a result, your child will want to devote time and energy to his or her career and put forward his or her best efforts, leading to a higher probability of success and a happier child.

Susan Jones recounts how her children's interest in musical instruments and acting from a young age created the fundamentals for a successful career in music. While raising her four daughters, Susan did not allow them to watch television and instead provided them with plenty of creative toys, sports equipment, and musical instruments. Her daughters gravitated toward performing by learning to play musical instruments and using the family video camera to make their own movies wearing Susan's high heels and clothes as costumes and using the family décor as props. It did not come as a surprise when three of her daughters eventually came together to form the country band the Lunabelles, after touring with Kenny Rogers for seven consecutive years, beginning when Susan's daughters were eight, ten, twelve, and fourteen years old. The daughters are now in their twenties and no longer performing as a group but still all actively writing and recording music. As opposed to many artists who begin their career at such a young age, Susan's daughters, the Arciero sisters, continued to hone their craft due to their love of their art and have received much respect and recognition from their peers.

Realistic Outlook

It is also important that you, as a parent, make sure that your child knows the realities of the music and entertainment business and is not motivated solely by fantasy. Visions of overnight success, money, cars, and glamour are misleading, and your child can be easily discouraged once he or she realizes that such is not the norm. Van Patten advises parents to "Tell it like it is: on the one hand it's a lot of hard work, some occasional sacrifices, and a fair amount of competition. On the other, it's the chance for a thrilling career, an invaluable growing experience, and, just possibly, financial security for life."[4] As a parent, it is important to be honest with your child. However, you must be careful not to discourage them by telling them that fame will *never* happen. True, you will want to protect your child from disappointment and the sometimes harsh realities of the music and entertainment industry, but it is crucial that you do not downplay their dreams. Your children must believe that greatness is possible in order to achieve it, and who better to instill this belief than a parent?

When assessing your child's level of motivation, make sure his or her enthusiasm is not just an effort to "please" you because your child knows it is what you want him or her to do. You must look past your own excitement to see whether your child is truly enjoying the pursuit of a career in music and entertainment or whether he or she is simply putting forth a "false face." After all, there is no one who knows your child better than you. That said, it may be natural for a child to be very motivated at the onset of his or her career path, then lose interest.

Pursuing a career in music and entertainment may become "no longer fun" as your child gets older. The further along the career path, the higher the level of competition, and the more effort and work is required from your child. Your child may find that he or she does not want to extend the extra efforts or that too many other "life things" are diverting his or her time and attention. Furthermore, the awkward transformations of puberty, such as voice changing, may affect your child's ability and confidence to perform and pursue a career in music and entertainment. This possible loss of interest makes it important to continually re-assess your child's motivation and interest throughout your journey to a successful career. Keep in mind, however, even if your child happens to outgrow his or her drive to pursue such a path, the journey, to that point, will have been a positive experience, full of enjoyment and life-long lessons in which your child will have learned something about him- or herself.

At what age should I allow my child to start pursuing a career?

This is a difficult question to answer, given that there is no "magical number" at which a child becomes "old enough" to enter the entertainment industry. All children grow and mature at different paces. Each child will differ in the ways he or she can handle pressure and face the challenges that will be presented to him or her within the entertainment industry. Though it is near impossible to pinpoint an exact age, generally you will want to begin your child's career when he or she is as old as possible. This will hopefully ensure maturity and an ability to understand and focus on the demands of the field. Some children are focused and prepared for anything at an early age. They know they want a career in entertainment, and they have eyes only for that. Others, however, will have a variety of interests, including entertainment, but no targeted interest in a career specifically in entertainment. If your child falls in the latter category, he or she is not yet ready to begin his or her career.

Susan Jones recalls the challenges her daughters faced when they first created the Lunabelles. Before touring with Kenny Rogers, they performed at local weddings, and the bride or party planner frequently presented them with a set list of up to forty songs. Therefore, the four girls, ranging between ages eight and fourteen, were challenged to learn an incredible amount of material in a very short period of time. Meeting these demands satisfied Susan that her girls were able to take on the responsibility of beginning a touring career at such a young age.

While Susan's youngest daughter was ready to hit the road as a musician at the age of eight, not every eight-year-old will have the maturity and ability to do so. This is generally an exceptionally young age at which to begin a career in music, and Susan's daughter's success may be attributed to the fact that she was accompanied by three older sisters. Cari Cole, a New York-based celebrity vocal coach and artist development specialist with thirty years of experience, states that the youngest client she has ever taken on was seven years old. She elaborates, however, that this was a rare exception she chose to make because of the talent and maturity demonstrated by that particular child. John Germain Leto, a New York-based image and life coach, works with motivated and mature child performers who are ready to assess their own creativity, and as a result, the youngest client he has coached was twelve years old. While some children are able to begin music careers at the age of seven or eight, such cases like those mentioned above are often the exception rather than the rule. That said, every situation should be evaluated on a case-by-case basis.

Another great concern in ensuring that your child is ready for a career in the music and entertainment industry is your child's ability to understand and handle rejection. Is your child still so young that, when rejected, she will be unable to understand that the rejection is no reflection on her self-worth, thus harming her self-esteem? If so, then your child is not yet old enough to handle a career in show business.

Breaking It Down

Some other factors to consider when deciding whether your child is "old enough" are the following:

1. How well can your child take instruction?

2. Does your child resist authority or have a tendency to "act out"?

3. Does he or she retract and shy away from people in new environments and situations?

4. Will he or she be able to handle rejection?

5. Is your child well socialized with other children?

6. Is he or she an exceptional reader and able to learn quickly?

7. Can he or she focus and be patient for long periods of time?

8. Can he or she occupy him- or herself during downtime?

9. Can your child understand the need for preparation and practice?

10. Can your child perform upon instruction?

11. Is your child capable of handling frequent commuting?

You must carefully observe your child's personality and actions. If he or she shows signs of an appropriate level of maturity and focus on entertaining, your child is "of age" and will be able to fully understand the demands of an entertainment career and rise to the level of professionalism and performance that is expected.

What legal issues should I be concerned with when planning my child's career?

Employment Laws

There are many legal safeguards in place to protect your child. Laws governing child labor, contracts, and education ensure your child's safety and health when working in the entertainment industry. Laws generally vary by state, the most notable of which are the child labor laws in California and New York. California labor law defines a minor as anyone under the age of eighteen who is required to attend school under the Education Code, and any other person under the age of six. The California Labor Code requires that all minors ages fifteen through eighteen employed in the entertainment industry have work permits. Similarly, all employers in the entertainment industry are required to obtain permits before employing minors. These permits may be obtained from the California Division of Labor Standards Enforcement.[5]

There are two types of permits issued to minors in the entertainment industry: individual permits and blanket permits. Individual permits are issued for six months to the minor specifically named in the application and must be renewed in the same manner and under the same conditions as the original permit. Blanket permits, on the other hand, are issued for groups of minors hired for special events or particular productions lasting a limited time. To obtain blanket permits, employers must prove that a parent or guardian will accompany each group of up to twenty minors.

New York's labor laws also provide for specific protection of children in the entertainment industry. Like California, New York requires that all employers of child performers obtain a Certificate of Eligibility to Employ Child Performers from the New York State Department of Labor. A parent or guardian of a child performer must obtain an Employment Permit for a Child Performer before their child begins working. This permit, which must be given to each employer, is valid for up to six months and must be renewed by a parent or guardian thirty days prior to expiration.[6]

Florida has also become a popular state for employment of child entertainers. Unlike California and New York, however, Florida does not require children to obtain permits before working. Employers, on the other hand, are required to obtain a Permit to Hire prior to employing any minor in Florida.

Education Laws

States have also enacted various education laws to ensure that child performers receive a satisfactory education while working. New York, for example, passed the Child Performer Education and Trust Act in 2003. This act requires that a parent or guardian provide evidence, each school semester, to the Department of Labor demonstrating that the child performer is maintaining satisfactory academic performance as determined by the child performer's school. Furthermore, it is the responsibility of the parent or guardian to ensure that the child goes no longer than ten consecutive days without educational instruction while the school of enrollment is in session.[7]

In addition to statutory regulations, if your child becomes a member of a union such as SAG-AFTRA, he or she will be further protected by union-mandated regulations. SAG-AFTRA, for example, has a specific committee, the Young Performers Committee, geared toward addressing the employment needs of young performers. All SAG-AFTRA members, regardless of the state of employment, are required to sign the SAG-AFTRA Theatrical/Television Contract. This contract includes specific mandates governing the employment of minors.[8] It stipulates that producers must notify the minor's parent of the terms and conditions of the minor's employment. If the minor is guaranteed three or more consecutive days of employment, the producer must hire a teacher, starting with the first day of the minor's employment, for any day on which the minor would normally be attending school. The minor must be taught an average of three hours a day, but no less than twenty minutes per day. SAG-AFTRA strongly promotes the importance of uninterrupted education, emphasizing that a young performer's education cannot be neglected by his or her pursuit of a career in entertainment.[9] Tess Filsoof, mother of child actress Rachel Filsoof, advises that a parent should always make sure school comes first. Because her daughter is an A/B student, she has been able to act in movies such as *Motion Music*, *Mean Girls 2*, *Tomorrow Comes Today*, and *Coffee and a Bite* since she was fourteen. In guiding her daughter in her career pursuits, Tess's approach reflects SAG-AFTRA's view on the importance of schooling and has allowed her daughter to become a well-educated and successful performer.

In addition to the above-mentioned mandates, SAG-AFTRA requires that union field representatives conduct periodic "spot checks" of sets on which SAG-AFTRA members, especially minors, are employed. These representatives monitor whether child performers are being asked to work overtime or beyond the permitted work hours; are getting adequate meal and rest periods; are being tutored in a safe and effective manner; are permitted to be within sight and sound of a parent or guardian at all times; have been provided an appropriate dressing room area; or have been asked to do hazardous work.[10]

Although these laws and regulations are in place, it is up to you as a parent to be vigilant and keep an eye out for any violations. If any laws are broken in the course of your child's employment, it is crucial that you act and report these violations. This requires you to be aware of the laws of the state your child is working in. Visit the state's website or other valid source to determine the laws in place to protect your child. By doing so, you will be better able to protect your child in his or her work environment.

Contract Law

During the course of your child's career, he or she will be required to enter into binding contracts, be it with a production company, manager, agent, producer, or record label. State laws also protect your child from becoming a victim of an unfair or fraudulent contract. Minors have the ability to void any contract they sign until they reach the age of majority.[11] This means that they will not be required to perform their side of the bargain if they so choose because the contract will not be legally binding on them. Most states (Florida, California, and New York included) require that entertainment contracts signed by a minor be approved by a judge before they are considered enforceable. Thus, most studios, record labels, or other employers will not sign a contract with your child without judicial approval.

To obtain judicial approval, an entity must first petition the court. The petition includes the crucial aspects of the contract: its duration (in terms of performances, time, etc.), the compensation to be paid, and what services both parties are providing.[12] The court will then review the petition and hold a hearing to ensure the child is not being exploited for financial gain. New York requires your child to be present at the hearing; however, this is not required by all states. (It is not a requirement, for example, in California.) During the hearing, the judge will ask questions to determine whether your child is exercising his or her own free will in choosing to pursue a career in entertainment and to what extent your child's "normal life" will be affected. Once satisfied that the contract is fair, freely entered into, and your child has been adequately protected, the court will approve the contract, making it legally binding upon your child.

Again, it is important that you, yourself, be aware of the contents of the contract so that you will recognize a breach of contract if one occurs. It will most likely be necessary for you to get an attorney to help you understand contract terms, as they can often be difficult to comprehend. The law is on your child's side, and you can rest assured that he or she is legally well-protected.

CHAPTER 2

Asking for Directions

What professionals do I need to hire to help guide my child's career?

THE ROAD TO A SUCCESSFUL career in entertainment can be hazardous, so you will need help in navigating its twists and turns. Assembling a team of experienced professionals will provide you with the guidance and "know-how" you need to help your child achieve his or her dream. The great triumvirate of your team includes a manager, agent, and attorney. These three professionals will take care of most of the business and legal aspects of your child's career and move him or her along the path to success. As discussed later on, a qualified accountant or business manager will also play an important role.

Agents and Managers

An agent will represent, advise, and solicit work for your child. He or she will also negotiate on your child's behalf in regards to employment. A manager will help develop and coordinate your child's career. If your child does not already have an agent, the manager will assist your child in finding one and serve as a liaison between your child and his or her agent. In forming these relationships, an attorney should be hired to review any contracts and negotiate their terms, ensuring that your child is legally protected in all respects.

Coaches

Other important members of your professional team may include vocal, acting, and dance coaches, producers, publicist, webmaster, and stylist.

It is important that your child continue to improve and develop his or her talents as their career progresses; thus, vocal, acting, and dance coaches are a key part of your child's career team. A publicist and webmaster will come in handy, along with photographers and videographers, to develop and promote your child's image and performances. They will also help you identify and build on an audience to create a demand for your child's performances.

Producers, Etc.

If your child is pursuing a career in the music business, it may be necessary to add additional professionals to your team. For example, it may help to hire a touring agent or performance consultant to secure shows and organize your child's travels among performances. A manager, or executive producer in the music business, will take care of the technical aspects of producing and recording your child's music. An experienced producer will help establish and stay true to your child's "sound and style" and should be someone your child feels comfortable working with. New York music producer Jimmy Landry of Cakewalk warns parents and their children against falling into the trap of getting involved with inexperienced producers. They often lack relationships to key industry professionals and the musical vocabulary required to complement your child's weaknesses. Due to their inexperience in the mainstream industry, he notes, "before you know it, your copyrights are tied to the producer and the material produced may require additional production later on."

Finding Your Team

When assembling your trusted professional team, look to trade publications or online directories for recommendations. Word of mouth within the industry is also a valuable source. However, before hiring anyone, make sure you thoroughly research each person to determine his or her legitimacy and ability. After researching the individual, conduct an interview to measure whether you, your child, and the potential "team member" will be able to work well together and form a trusting and respectful business relationship. Voice coach Trapper Felides sums up the process of assembling your child's professional team as follows: "It's a puzzle, not a hierarchy or meritocracy. You need the right fit, not only the best talent."

What is the difference between an agent and a manager?

Agents

While there is some overlap, your child's agent and manager perform significantly different roles. An agent's primary purpose is to seek out job opportunities for your child. They communicate with casting directors and record executives to help coordinate and schedule auditions and performances. Agents are required to be licensed by the state. A professional agent will not ask for money in advance but will require a 10 percent (more or less) commission once your child makes money off of a job. Agent Halle Madia recommends starting with a smaller agent when beginning your career. That agent will have more time and energy to devote to your child who is just entering the business and trying to build a résumé of experience. All in all, finding a trustworthy and reliable agent is crucial in your child's path to show business success, as he or she will be the key to finding jobs.

Managers

A manager works with you and your child on a more personal level, handling many personal and day-to-day aspects of your child's career pursuits. He or she will more likely have fewer clients to attend to than would an agent and will therefore have a more hands-on approach to handling your child's career. Personal managers take stock of your child's strengths and weaknesses in performing and ensure that your child is reaching his or her full potential. They serve as a career counselor and image consultant, assess proper roles, long-term benefits, or detriments of certain career moves and help you in building up your child's confidence. Although managers will not directly submit your child for an audition, they may act as a liaison between your child and his or her agent, ensuring that the over-burdened agent is putting enough effort into soliciting job opportunities and that your son or daughter is prepared for each audition. If your child does not already have an agent, a manager can be a valuable resource in helping your child obtain one due to his or her extensive industry contacts.

In addition to a talent or personal manager, you may want to retain a separate business manager. As discussed later on, business managers will make sure bills and tax obligations are attended to and account for all income and expenditures, while personal managers will keep track of your child's schedule and day-to-day activities and needs.

How do I select the professionals who will be helping to further my child's career?

Managers

Securing a qualified manager is an important first step. The manager will have the bandwidth and ability to collaborate with you about your child's potential and career path. The manager can also be instrumental to securing a talent agent. Because you and your child will work so closely with a manager, it is important to have a solid relationship of mutual trust and respect. Managers often become "like one of the family" and develop a personal interest in your child's success. Manager Eileen DeNobile stresses that she has faith in her clients, and likewise, her clients are loyal to her because they have developed that essential sense of respect and know she is putting forth her best efforts to advance their career. The development of this type of relationship makes the process of choosing a manager key.

The best attribute to a potential manager's character is a positive referral. Recommendations by others in the industry, be they other performers or your entertainment attorney, will help you judge whether your child's best interests will be served by that manager and whether your child and the manager (and you!) will be able to form a trusting relationship. After compiling a list of managers, attempt to schedule interviews. Once you accomplish this difficult task (as good managers are usually extremely busy), be sure that you and your child treat this interview as you would any other audition or job interview. After all, your child is trying to "sell" him- or herself to the manager, just as much as you and your child are "auditioning" the manager to check for a good fit. Be sure to ask appropriate questions relating to the manager's prior experience, types of clients, charges (usually 10 to 20 percent), and the types of services the manager will perform.

During and after the interview, pay close attention to your child's reaction to meeting the manager. Ask your child what he or she thinks of the manager and how he or she would feel about working with them. After all, your child will be the one working closely with the manager, and you want to ensure that your child feels comfortable with that person. Eileen DeNobile emphasizes that she maintains positive working relationships and open lines of communication with both her child clients and their parents because professional parents and their child come together and work as a team. It is only when all parties trust each other and work together that your child's career will flourish and benefit from bringing a manager onboard.

Agents

It becomes helpful to employ the services of an agent as soon as your child is ready to look for work. As previously discussed, a manager can introduce you and your child to qualified agents. When searching for an agent, it is important to find one with whom your child feels comfortable enough to grow to trust and take direction from. Because an agent will be searching for and booking your child's jobs, it is crucial that he or she get to know your child fairly well on a personal and professional level. This will ensure that the kind of work the agent is booking is appropriate for your child and something your child's talents and personality are well suited for.

The first step in searching for an agent is to compile a list of reputable agents and agencies in your region. It is unwise to hire anyone other than a franchised agent, who is approved by and subject to the rules of one of the three performing arts unions. The three major talent unions, SAG (Screen Actors Guild), AFTRA (American Federation of Television and Radio Artists), and AEA (Actors' Equity Association), publish the names of reputable agents in their newsletters. You can also obtain a list of franchised agents in major cities, such as New York and Los Angeles, by obtaining a copy of the *Ross Reports Television & Film*, a monthly trade publication that provides the names of franchised talent agents. If you do not live in or near a major city, you can contact a local television station or advertising agency to find out who supplies them with their young talent.

Once you have compiled your list, the next step is to solicit their representation. Mail your child's headshot to each agent listed with a list of your child's "vital information" and attributes stapled to the back. Such a list should contain contact information, age, height, weight, coloring, talents, and any experience in show business or experience related thereto (such as school plays and music/dance/acting lessons).[13] Include with your child's headshot a *brief* (no more than three paragraphs) note to the agent explaining that you are seeking representation for your child. Include any supplemental recordings if your child is a singer. In this new age of technology, you may be tempted to simply email the agents with attachments. Unless specified (on a website or after a phone call regarding submissions), it is not advisable to send your child's information to an agent in this manner. Agents are very busy people and receive a barrage of emails every day. The chances that your submission will be lost in the shuffle or accidentally deleted are high. It is therefore best to send a physical copy of the materials to the agent to ensure a better chance that the agent will receive and consider them.

The next step in finding an agent is to be patient. Agents who are interested in representing your child will contact you to set up an interview. It may be several weeks before you receive a response from an agent. Making follow-up phone calls after one or two weeks may help speed the process along or remind the agent that he or she needs to look at your child's submission and get back to you.

Once you have scheduled an interview, treat it as if it were an audition. During the interview, your child will be asked to accompany the agent to his or her office without you. This, in essence, is the first "test" of whether your child is "worthy" of representation. If your child is uncomfortable separating from you for this interview, the agent will assume that he or she will be unable to do so for an audition, and thus, conclude that your child is not ready for show business. During the interview, the agent will undoubtedly converse with your child and ask him or her questions both related and unrelated to his or her career path. Your child needs to exude confidence, poise, and personality. The agent will be assessing your child's character to determine if he or she is cut out for a career in show business and is someone they can and would want to work with. Former talent agent Halle Madia notes that she looked for children who were in her office because of their own interest in the business, as opposed to those who were over-coached by their parents. This personal motivation will be evident in a child's initial interactions with the agent.

If your child is looking to get into acting, the agent will have him or her read an excerpt from a script and act it out. For children who are not yet able to read, an agent will usually make up a situation and have the child "pretend" along with them to assess his or her acting abilities and how well the child can take direction.

Once the interview is over, if the agent is interested in representing your child, the agent will want to meet with you. Believe it or not, you, too, are being "interviewed" by the agent to see whether you will be a pain or a pleasure to work with. Because an agent will undoubtedly have much interaction with you, the parent, he or she will want to make sure that you will not pose a problem by being too overbearing and difficult to work with (especially in the case of young children).

Although it is important for the agent to "like" your child, it is equally as important for your child to feel comfortable with the agent. After the interview, ask your child how he or she felt about the agent and what his or her thoughts were about the interview. Furthermore, you must feel that the agent is competent and reliable and will be a benefit to your child's career. The agent must impress you, as well. Have some questions ready for the agent when it is your turn to meet with him or her. Find out the agent's thoughts on your child's potential for success and what type of work he or she plans to pursue for your child. Don't be afraid to ask for a list of the agent's former and current clients and find out what casting directors the agents have a working relationship with in order to check out how well "connected" the agent is. Finally, assess how well *you* can communicate with the agent. With such an active role in your child's career, it is crucial that you and the agent are able to work together as "partners" in helping your child achieve success in show business.

Can I be my own child's manager?

Managing your child's career is very tricky and often discouraged by industry professionals. The role of manager requires a high degree of insider industry know-how. Professional business managers are well versed in the intricacies of the business and have already established the industry relationships that are crucial to achieving a successful career. Furthermore, by becoming your child's manager, you are taking on an entirely new career in itself that will require a majority of your time and energy. Unless you are an experienced professional in this realm of business yourself, you and your child would probably benefit most from hiring an independent personal manager.

If you still want to have some active involvement in the management of your child's career, you may want to serve as part of the management team, perhaps in the role of management coordinator. This will enable you to have a say in any material decisions, but there will still be deference to a manager's judgment and expertise. Such a management hierarchy will prevent any mistaken career moves that you, the inexperienced manager-parent, may have taken if managing on your own. As stated by Dick Van Patten and Peter Berk, "A wrong move now could jeopardize your child's career before it even gets off the ground."[14]

Despite such warnings, some parents may find it difficult to share the steering wheel with a manager at the very beginning of the journey. Even in these cases, it is crucial that you draw up a management agreement addressing every issue you would want set forth in an agreement with outside managers. There are a plethora of horror stories involving parental mismanaging of their child's career, and you will want to make sure that your child's story does not join the ranks. For further reference, this is specifically addressed in Section 2, "Essential Terms of a Management Agreement" in the Operating Manual appendix at the back of this book.

Should I consult a lawyer before signing a contract with an agent or manager on behalf of my child?

The simple, resounding answer to this question is "YES." When an agent concludes that he or she is interested in representing your child, the agent will often give you a standard agency contract to review and sign. A manager may also give you his or her own standard management company agreement. These documents will undoubtedly be biased in the agent's or manager's favor and may provide little protection for your child. To ensure your child is entering into a fair business arrangement, it is crucial that you have a specialized entertainment lawyer look over the contracts before signing. No matter how much the agent or manager pressures you, you are under no obligation to sign immediately. (In fact, pressure to do so may be a sign that there is something "fishy" about the contract and provide even more incentive to have it reviewed by an attorney.)

Choosing a Lawyer

Finding the right attorney is much like finding the right doctor. Like doctors, there are lawyers who specialize in certain areas of law. You will need someone who not only deals frequently with contracts, but also is well-versed in the language of entertainment contracts and intellectual property. Entertainment lawyers are skilled in the practice of negotiating show business contracts and will know what "red flag" provisions to look out for that could potentially harm your child's career. They can skillfully assert your child's interests and negotiate revisions to the agreement that are to your child's benefit or to the mutual benefit of your child and the manager/agent.

The easiest way to find a good entertainment attorney is by a referral from a contact you have in show business or from another attorney. If you do not have any such resources, you can contact the bar association of the nearest large city for a list of members belonging to their entertainment divisions. It may also be beneficial to get the names of some attorneys in one of the two main hubs of the entertainment world, New York and Los Angeles, as lawyers from those areas are likely to have the most experience with entertainment contracts and be the "best in the business."

When selecting a lawyer, remember to assess his or her qualifications. Find out what types of clients the lawyer represents, how many years of experience he or she has in the entertainment industry, and how fees will be calculated. Usually, an attorney will not charge to meet with you for the initial assessment of how and if he or she can work with you and your child, but it is always best to ask to confirm such consultation is free of charge. Generally, once you begin to discuss substantive legal issues, the lawyer may begin to charge you for his or her time. It is thus beneficial to discuss costs at the beginning of the meeting to ensure that there are no misunderstandings at the end.

Financial Concerns

You may be reluctant to hire an attorney because of the costs associated with legal services. Although a good entertainment attorney's hourly rate is definitely not cheap, in the big picture, it is a small price to pay to ensure the security of your child's professional career. Many lawyers may offer flat fees for contract review or hour-long consultations during which he or she will address any legal concerns you may have. If you make your financial constraints known to the attorney, he or she may be able to work out a more beneficial fee arrangement with you. This ability, however, may depend on the firm's policies on fee agreements and the lawyer's status within the firm. If obtaining an entertainment attorney is still outside of your financial means, contact the Volunteer Lawyers for the Arts (VLA) organization in the big city nearest to you. If you meet the financial restrictions for their legal services, your local VLA will refer you to a qualified attorney who has experience in arts-related issues who can help you at little to no cost.

Does my child need an attorney for anything besides contract review?

The road to your child's success in show business is full of potholes and unexpected turns. Your child will encounter many legal issues that do not directly involve the review and negotiation of contracts for which you will need a lawyer's services. For example, a lawyer will be able to advise you on how to comply with the child labor laws of the state your child will be working in and assist your child in obtaining a work permit to give your child permission to work. Furthermore, a seasoned entertainment lawyer may be helpful in finding an agent or manager if your child does not already have one. Entertainment lawyers, especially those in major entertainment cities such as New York and Los Angeles, are generally well connected and have many valuable contacts within the industry. In such areas, entertainment lawyers may also provide strategic services that overlap with some of the role of a manager, reducing the immediate need to hire someone for that position.

Consulting your lawyer for every release or basic industry transaction form you have to sign will prove extremely costly, but not to consult a lawyer may prove even more costly in the event of a conflict or "contract gone bad." To help mitigate the costs, you should explore the possibility of a contingency compensation arrangement to have your counsel receive a percentage of revenues earned. Unless your child generates sufficient income from a high volume of contracts and business transactions, your lawyer may be reluctant to agree to be compensated in this manner. However, if he or she does, it will provide you with significant savings in up-front costs. Regardless of the compensation model, be prudent of how you use your lawyer's services. Never attempt to make important and complex legal decisions without him or her!

Once my child's career is underway, what other team members should I employ to enhance it?

Publicist

When your child's career has taken off, and he or she begins to gain public notoriety, it may be time to enlist the services of a publicist. A publicist will help maintain and promote your child's professional image to the public. Prematurely obtaining a publicist, however, will do you little good, as oftentimes a qualified publicist will not have the time or ability to build a public image for your child from scratch. Typically, you will want to wait until your child has obtained a notable or recurring role that has put him or her in the public eye. Ask yourself, "Has my child played a role/had a hit song that is enough of a 'big deal' to make the public take notice?" Making sure that the answer is "yes" will give the publicist a jumping-off point for promoting your child in the context of his or her career. Your child will benefit very little from having his or her public image managed if he or she does not yet have one.

Once you have determined that your child has secured notable employment, enough to put him or her in the public eye, a publicist will further that image by attracting attention through various media outlets. Your child's publicist will help create a campaign that will be best tailored to your child's needs and may include press releases, endorsements, talk show interviews, magazine articles, photo opportunities, and public appearances. However, just as with every other professional you hire to help further your child's career, it is important that you first interview the publicist to ensure he or she fully understands the path your child wants his or her career to take. You will also want to research the candidate to ensure he or she is someone with a good reputation within the industry and is well connected to reputable media outlets.

Digital Marketing Consultant

Given the growing significance of digital platforms and social media, you will want to enlist the services of a digital marketing professional. Often provided as part of the publicity services, a digital marketing consultant will coordinate with you and your webmaster to create and disseminate digital content such as photos, videos, and music files. They will also help you identify and build your child's fan base, which can be an asset to promote your child's projects.

Business Manager

Another team member that may be of value once your child begins to book steady and well-paying work is the business manager. Once your child's income reaches about $50,000 per year, a business manager will be useful in managing your child's finances. Business managers tend to be certified public accountants who have experience dealing with the financial matters of the entertainment industry. A business manager will perform such services as maintaining financial records, paying bills, banking, and filing your child's tax returns. He or she may also create and maintain trust accounts for your child so that your child's future is financially secure. Like attorneys, business managers can be expensive. They charge an hourly fee or a percentage of your child's annual income. Regardless of the expense, it is essential that you consult with a specialized accountant or business manager to establish an appropriate approach to handling the costs, income, and taxes associated with your child's career.

Creative Team

Your child may also benefit from having a team of creative instructors to guide and condition them along the way. As mentioned in a previous section, such a "creative team" may include an acting, vocal, or dance coach, and a master producer (if your child is a music artist). The need for these team members will become obvious when your child's career reaches a certain stage. These people will generally be professionals with whom your child has worked in the past and feels comfortable enough to have and want with him or her at all times.

CHAPTER 3

Hitting the Road

What basic "first steps" should I take to prepare for facilitating my child's career?

PREPARATION IS THE KEY TO success once you and your child make the decision to pursue a career in entertainment. Without adequate preparation for the journey into the industry, your child will almost certainly never leave the driveway—much less make it to the fast track on the highway to stardom. Look at it from this perspective: even if you have a Ferrari, without gas in the tank and knowledge of your destination, it is impossible to drive anywhere.

Training and Experience

When going on a long trip, it is best to fuel the car before you leave. The fuel for your child's career is experience: a résumé must be built from the ground up. In order to secure parts in the entertainment industry, your child must develop skills that only instruction and experience can provide. Casting directors can sense a first-time amateur as soon as they walk through the door. There is no reason to waste their time or yours by putting your child in a situation in which rejection is the only possible outcome. Get your child some professional instruction from a music teacher, acting coach, singing instructor, or any other experienced professional in the field your child wants to enter. Resist the temptation to simply pick the most convenient name out of the phonebook. If you live near a major city, take your child there to find and meet a qualified instructor. Seeking a well-regarded and experienced coach will pay dividends both in the quality of instruction that your child receives and in the relationship that the instructor will have to other professionals within the industry. A good instructor will not only help your child realize his or her potential but may facilitate opportunities and contacts for it as well.

In addition to professional instruction, activities such as involvement in the school drama club, community theater, or other performance group is an easy way to gain experience and build a résumé early on. Performance in such groups will not only hone skills but will help to acclimate a child to performing in front of large crowds of complete strangers and give your child an opportunity to showcase his or her talent.

After-school, acting schools and/or summer performing arts camps are also good options for getting your child both professional instruction and performance experience to build a résumé. As an added bonus, they can also give your child the opportunity to expand socially and meet same-age kids with similar interests. Ron Schaefer, director of French Woods Camp for forty-five years and counting, explains that camps like his allow children interested in acting, singing, and dancing to audition for musicals to see where they stand among their peers. If the child lands a leading role, he or she will realize that they can compete with kids his or her own age and obtain the training necessary to land professional roles. On the other hand, if a child auditions and consistently ends up in the ensemble, he or she may be talented yet lack what it takes to succeed in the highly competitive music and entertainment industry.[15] In addition to being a lot of fun, attending a performing arts summer camp can provide your child with many valuable lessons, which may prepare him or her for what can be expected in a career in the music and entertainment industry.

Résumés, Etc.

When first compiling your child's résumé, there will most likely not be much work experience to put on there, which is why taking the steps relating to instruction and performance listed above are so important. You should also list any school or extra-curricular acting, singing, or theater experience that your child has aside from any professional instruction they are undergoing. Once your child has gone on some auditions (and hopefully landed some parts), you can update the résumé with those jobs and experiences as they occur.

The next item you will need for the journey is a headshot of your child. Headshots are not simply photos of your child's face that you can take at home. The headshot is usually the first thing that a casting director or agent sees, so the picture must clearly make a good impression. Good headshots do so in a way that shows a glimpse of the child's talent or highlights his or her best features. Bear in mind, however, that you should not spend thousands of dollars on headshots. Children grow rapidly, so be prepared to update your child's headshot on annual basis. Agents and managers see prospective clients every day based on digital photos. Therefore, your child does not need a professional picture to get into the business. Eventually, when your child's career has progressed to regular auditions and castings, it may make more sense to invest in headshots.

Keep in mind through all of this that you should hold true to the basic principle that your child's career is a business. Putting in valuable time, effort, and research into selecting the correct instructor, camp, or school will ensure the greatest benefit and a maximum return on your money. Devoting more time to the search will also help you avoid scams and inexperienced instructors. Do not be afraid to ask for references or speak to people who have used the instructor to ensure that the person is the best fit for your child.

As you will undoubtedly begin to see, it takes a tremendous amount of time and effort to give your child a chance to succeed in the entertainment industry. When taking these preliminary steps on the long road to success, always keep your child's desires in mind. If they are not interested in putting in the effort, it probably is not worth it to force them. The road is too long and challenging to push them all the way there. Show business is just that—a business—but do not forget that you are a good parent first and a good business advisor second.

How can I get my child an audition?

The car has gas and is ready to go, but what is the destination? It is impossible for your child to secure a career-making role if you are unaware of the time and location of auditions. The first and easiest way to locate auditions is to search for them online. Certain websites, such as *Backstage*, offer the times, locations, and descriptions of auditions for a membership fee, but a simple Google search is often enough to locate auditions. You can also monitor community message boards and local papers, as all might have information on auditions. If you live in or near a major city, *Variety* and the entertainment section of the local papers have audition news as well. However, if you choose to go this route, be selective. Make sure that the description of the part matches your child's physical appearance and skill set. If it does not, you are not only wasting the casting director's time but your child's and your own as well. Acting consultant, actress, and producer Emily Grace suggests that parents and their children zero-in on certain types of work, such as commercials or television. She warns, "It's hard to create momentum when you're throwing spaghetti against the wall to see what will stick." Thus, find out what specific area of entertainment your child is most interested in and best suited for, and actively pursue that direction.

Keep in mind that your child may well audition for a casting director on multiple occasions. Casting director Beth Melsky warns parents that in a six-month cycle, she may see a child numerous times. Beginning your relationship by annoying the casting director is not a good way to jumpstart a career. As is the case with agent and manager interviews mentioned in the previous section, you, the parent, are also, in a way, auditioning and can affect your child's chances of landing a job. Beth's fellow casting director, Adrienne Stern, advises parents that their reputation and behavior on the set may determine whether or not their children work again. It is widely understood that children whose parents have fits, boast to everyone about his or her child's contract and compensation, or otherwise cause trouble on the set might have no chance of succeeding in the entertainment industry. Adrienne has also witnessed many parents jeopardize their child's career based on their own control issues and tendency to be overbearing. Despite producers' sympathy for talented children with overbearing parents, if the parent is too much of a problem, they will not work with the child.

The task of finding auditions is not completely on your shoulders, however. Once your child has acquired an agent, it is the agent's job to find work for your child. He or she will not only help you find open auditions but will select the more desirable jobs that will prove most beneficial to your child's career. He or she will know which auditions to send your child out to and, perhaps equally important, which auditions you should pass on.

How do I prepare my child for an audition?

Preparation is the key to a successful audition. As emphasized before, an audition is a job interview and needs to be treated as such. Simply walking in and "winging it" leaves your child's chances of landing the role very low in a case where odds of success are poor to begin with. Some agents, however, discourage young actors from over-preparing for auditions. The key is to ensure your child maintains his or her "natural demeanor" and lets his or her personality shine through. Clouding your child's character by over-preparing may make your child come off fake or forced.

Before the Audition

Manager Eileen DeNobile breaks down a child's approach to auditioning into five simple steps:

1. Walk in.

2. Do the best you can.

3. Walk out.

4. Don't think about the audition ever again (unless the manager receives feedback and the child is over twelve).

5. Go home and play with your friends.

As you will often find in entertainment, information is your most valuable tool. If possible, seek out any information you can get on the part your child is auditioning for from your agent, manager, or the casting director. If you have all the information on the part and on what your child will be asked to do at the audition, your child will be much better prepared to handle what is coming down the road.

If possible, hire a dramatic or vocal coach to help prepare your child for the audition. Ask them if they have had other kids audition for the particular casting director that is running the audition. The coach should be able to provide advice on what casting directors look for and will help structure the practice sessions to get the most value out of the time put in. If possible, videotape the practice performance and let your child watch it. Allowing them to see their performance from the vantage point of an observer rather than a performer can visually illustrate flaws that would otherwise be difficult for a child to comprehend and correct.

There are many professional acting and vocal coaches who may further help your child hone his or her talents in preparation for an important audition. Each instructor often has his or her own unique teaching style. Ken Feinberg, an acting coach and founder of his own training studio in Atlanta, coaches many students through what he calls their "ET," which stands for emotional transition and pertains to the emotions associated with an actor's delivery, even if it is only one line. For example, a student once met with Ken to prepare for a one-liner audition for the television show *The Vampire Diaries* and landed the role because he was able to convey the emotions associated with that single line. New York-based performance coach, Ilyana Kadushin, who also has experience as a performer and voice-over artist, teaches based on the alchemical precept, "through repetition, the magic is forced to rise." Ilyana imparts this quote on her students in order to underscore how potent practice, discipline, and experience can be for an aspiring young performer.

Having coaches prepare your child for auditions will not only improve your child's chances of success because of heightened skills but will also improve your child's confidence and state of mind when going through the auditioning process. In the music arena, vocal coach Cari Cole seeks to do more than simply improve an aspiring pop star's singing. She builds confidence in young artists and helps them develop a personal identity from which they can create their own brand. This confidence is a crucial quality that raises the potential of every audition.

Dancer, choreographer, and artist development specialist Brian Thomas recognizes the importance of having your child connect with a casting director and convey to him or her that your child will be able to similarly connect with an audience. Brian helps young artists improve their ability to do so by training them to establish a rapport, share in the energy, stay in the moment, maintain focus and balance, and practice.

At the Audition

There are several things to do on the day of the audition that are vital to your child's success. First, make sure that your child dresses appropriately for the audition. This does not mean that slacks and a button-down shirt are your only option. It would still be appropriate to vary the attire based upon the part and the show. If, for example, the audition is for the part of a laid-back, casually dressed character, then jeans may be perfectly acceptable. There may be temptation to send your child in costume: resist this temptation at all costs. Unless the casting director specifically asks, do not dress your child in costume as it only makes them seem less professional and detracts from the performance.

Second, do not take chances with the part. Gather as much information as you can on how it is usually played and have your child play it to the best of his or her ability. Be conservative; this is not the time to take bold risks, as doing so only shows a casting director something he or she was not looking to see. Casting directors audition hundreds of children for a part and are usually looking for very specific qualities. Let your child's talent speak for itself as opposed to trying to catch the casting director's eye with an unusual change or gimmick. The risk simply is not worth the nearly nonexistent prospect of reward. By understanding what to expect at an audition, your child will increase his or her chances of landing a role or gig, thus advancing his or her career down the path to show business success.

Will I be allowed on-set/on-site with my child?

Parents are allowed on-set or on-site with their child if he or she is a minor. An adult guardian is permitted, if not required, to be with the child while on-set. However, it is important for you to be receptive to changes in your child's needs. Some children benefit from having their parent on-set; others may cling to a parent and have difficulty working when the parent is present. If this is the case, you must be willing to step back and allow someone whom both you and your child trust to fill the role of on-set guardian, such as a manager or other family member. It will undoubtedly be difficult at first, but realize that in the long-term it will be a boon to your child's career and allow your child to develop a sense of independence as well.

CHAPTER 4

Paying the Tolls

SHOULD YOU AND YOUR CHILD embark on this journey, one unavoidable consideration is how the trip will be financed. Your child's venture into the entertainment industry can be expensive. Costs will be incurred on many fronts: instructors, tutors and professional advisors, and a publicist will require financial compensation—not to mention the basic everyday living and traveling expenses that go hand-in-hand with your child's unique career choice. Naturally, you may well wonder if you can afford these expenses and where you can find the money to ensure that your child can pursue his or her dream. Rest assured that while it may not always be easy, there are steps you can take to secure the financial backing you and your child need to launch his or her career.

How do I find the finances to pay for everything?

Piecing together the financial backing to get the ball rolling on your child's career may not be easy, but it is not impossible, either. One of the first things you need to do is to craft a business plan based on your and your child's definition of "success." Only then can you realistically determine what costs you will have to pay and how you can keep them to a minimum. The easiest way you can do that is to start by creating a budget. A budget will allow you to determine precisely how much money you will need to spend to facilitate your child's career objectives. Once you have that number, you can make a determination on your ability to fund your child's career yourself. If you find that you simply do not have the funds, however, then it is time to consider alternative financing options.

In considering alternative ways to finance your child's career in entertainment, return to the principle that this is a business, and your child's career requires investment capital. You may have to turn to family, friends, and supporters in search of lenders or potential investors. This can be difficult, but so long as you spell out both your and your funder's financial expectations in detail, you will be able to avoid the misunderstandings that often plague these business and personal relationships. Your legal counsel can prepare appropriate investment and loan agreements that will provide cash flow in exchange for proceeds earned from your child's prospective career.

The need for detail and realism, however, cannot be understated. Include a payment schedule that spells out the money you receive up front and the sums or percentages of revenue to be paid in return and when these sums or percentages are to be paid back to the investor. Detail precisely the return the investors should expect on their investment if and when your child's career becomes a success. The same applies to loans. Try to be inclusive. The fewer details included in the agreement, the lower the likelihood that the deal will come to a successful conclusion. Although the investment documents will contain risk warnings, be sure to discuss the potential financial risks with your investors. Should you borrow money, you must outline the risk of default on payment if your child's career simply does not blossom the way that you imagined it will.

In addition to securing capital through debt or equity, many artists today are financing their career costs through digital crowdfunding platforms, such as Kickstarter, Indiegogo, Pledge Music, and Patreon. This trending practice also serves as a useful method to introduce a new artist to fans in order to build an audience. As discussed below, the crowdfunding artist creates and presents a video seeking financial support. Rather than incur a financial obligation to the supporter, the artist offers merchandise (such as music, posters, or t-shirts) or services (such as performances or personal appearances).

None of this is easy to do. This must be understood from the start. Launching your child's career is not unlike launching any new business. If you want to use the turnpike, you have to pay the tolls. The more money you are able to raise, the fewer back roads you will have to use and the faster you will be able to vault your child's career forward.

What should I include when creating my budget?

Creating a budget helps you understand all the tolls you will have to pay. The costs of jump-starting a career in music and entertainment can be expensive. To appreciate the costs associated with launching your child's career as a young actor, consider the following categories when creating your budget: vocal, talent, and dance coaching, transportation to auditions, head shots, photography, publicity, digital marketing, video production and editing, website design and maintenance, and performing arts camp.

If your child is focused on a prospective career within the music business, the sample estimated budget below may be used as a rough guide:

Recording studio costs, producing and musician fees, studio and sound engineer fees, reproduction costs	$25,000 (EP*)-$50,000 (CD)
Website design and maintenance	$5,000
Marketing and promotion costs (digital marketing, video promotion, etc.)	$7,500
Publicist	$10,000
Travel, transport, meals, etc.	$5,000
Styling, costume, hair & makeup	$2,500
Instructors (dance/vocal/musical instruments)	$2,500-$5,000
Video production and photography	$5,000-$10,000

*An EP is an abbreviated compilation consisting of three to six recordings.

Totaling those costs, you may need to raise in the range of $50,000 or higher to cover the initial costs to launch your child's music career. That can certainly be a daunting figure, but you must work intelligently and creatively to give your child the tools he or she will need to succeed in the industry.

How can I ensure that my child appreciates and understands the significance of the money he or she earns and is unaffected by his or her financial success?

This aspect of your child's career path is deeply personal and particularly challenging. For your child to have longevity, you have to ensure that your child stays grounded. Keeping your child in the loop on expenses is a key component in getting him or her to understand the significance of the money he or she earns. Another way to do this is to keep your child in his or her natural environment. For as long as possible, it is recommended that you resist the temptation to privately tutor or home school your child. Instead, seek to preserve his or her comfort zone by keeping your child in school with friends and classmates. The lessons your child will learn outside of the classroom in the social context of grade school can be as valuable as what they learn from their teachers during class. Your child will be influenced by the attitudes of children his or her age who are not making an income and come to realize that his or her situation is truly unique and that to have the money he or she makes is a special privilege. This type of education can help give your child the foundation he or she needs to be able to appreciate that the money he or she will earn is not to be taken for granted.

The opportunity to share common experiences with nonprofessional children your child's age will also help steer him or her clear of the hazards that exist when most of his or her time is occupied in show business. Many child performers have complicated family involvements with different goals. To avoid the risk of exposure to negative values, prudent parents monitor the time their child spends with other child entertainers. A good way to balance the competing interests here is to allow your child to attend a performing arts summer camp while still enrolling in a normal school during the year. Doing so provides your child an opportunity to develop friendships with other creative children while lowering the risk of overexposure.

It is vital that you instill within your child the sense that his or her career is a fun elective activity, not your child's primary responsibility. Should your child land a part or achieve similar success, do not treat him or her like a celebrity. If a biography needs to be written for your child, work with him or her to do it together as opposed to simply writing it for your child. Maintain the practice of giving your child domestic responsibilities or chores. If the child disregards them, explain that his or her career is a bonus, not a necessity. What you must impress upon your child is that school and family come first and his or her career second. If your child cannot handle all of these responsibilities at once, you need to be the parent and have the strength to reduce or remove the career from your child's life. If not, your child will be riding in a car in which the driver has taken his or her eye off the road: the car will rapidly career out of control.

Finally, even if your child has balanced work with school well, you need to pull the plug if your child is unable or unwilling to treat his or her career professionally. If your child is unprepared for auditions or rehearsals, put a stop to things immediately. Your child's chosen trade is a difficult one; it requires far too much time, energy, and hard work to succeed without complete dedication. If you do not teach your child to respect it as a professional opportunity, it is unlikely that he or she ever will. Do not allow your child to waste the other performers' and directors' time by giving matters short shrift. Instead, teach your child to respect his or her own performances and the others they work with. Doing so will greatly increase your child's chance of success in the entertainment industry and keep him or her firmly rooted in reality.

What can I do to make sure that my child's finances are secure for the future?

The best way to secure your child's financial future is to locate a qualified accountant or business manager that you can trust. One of the most common mistakes that people make in this situation is to simply select a family member to handle the financial aspects of the child's career. It cannot be stated more plainly than this: avoid doing this at all costs. You and your family should not be investing for your child or managing his or her taxes. Seek out experienced advisors that have solid credentials and references whom you feel you can trust. If at all possible, secure both a business manager and an investment advisor to make responsible tax decisions and long-term investments with your child's earnings.

Accountant and business manager Barry Klarberg recommends that parents first familiarize themselves with a prospective accountant's or business manager's professional history, client representations, and qualifications as a Certified Public Accountant (CPA) before hiring such individual as an accountant or business manager. Moreover, Klarberg promotes the idea of a brief "try out" period before you make a long-term commitment by signing an accountant's or business manager's contract.

This important piece of advice will enable you and your child to walk away if necessary without any financial "strings attached" as your child's career takes off. Klarberg also emphasizes the need to understand all other aspects of the arrangement between you, your child, and your business manager. Here, as mentioned in an earlier chapter, is where having an attorney to review such agreements will come into play. Finally, Klarberg urges parents to maintain control of signature authority and not be so quick to provide financial advisors with powers of attorney.

Financing your child's career can be complicated. It can be easy to get caught up in the costs and what you feel you need the money for. Finding a qualified accountant or business manager who is accustomed to dealing with entertainers can help you simplify matters and make sound financial decisions based upon what is best for your child in the long term.

What laws are in place to govern and protect my child's income?

Once your child begins to bring in revenue, those earnings must be handled in a specific way in accordance with relevant trust laws. Parents in New York, California, Louisiana, and New Mexico must establish a locked trust account for their child and provide the corresponding account number to their child's employer prior to obtaining a work permit.[16] At that point, the employer is required to withhold 15 percent of the minor's gross wages and deposit such amount into the trust account within fifteen days of employment.

These laws originated from a situation encountered by Jackie Coogan, a child film actor of the 1920s who made an unfortunate discovery on his twenty-first birthday that the earnings he worked so hard for as a child had been depleted. Under California law at the time, the earnings of minors belonged to their parents. As a result of Jackie's unfortunate experience, the Coogan Law was adopted to protect young actors' financial futures.

Accountant and business manager, Barry Klarberg refers to the Coogan Law as "a checks and balances system, which prevents abuse by parents and others representing minors." In California, parents are required to open a Coogan Account, or locked trust account, at a

California bank. Parents in New York and Louisiana are required to open similar accounts, but such accounts may be opened with a bank in any state. In New Mexico, locked trust accounts are only required if the child earns over $1,000 on an employment contract.

These locked trust accounts are controlled by a trustee, who can be anyone from a parent to an attorney, but the money within it can only be accessed by the minor upon turning eighteen or with a court order. Again, this is done as a protective measure to ensure that child performers do not reach adulthood only to see that their earnings have been squandered for them. Note that 15 percent is the minimum amount that must be put into the account. If you can afford to do so, it is advisable to put a higher percentage into the account to ensure more is saved for your child once he or she reaches adulthood. Though this can be difficult to do, especially given the high costs associated with starting your child's career, in the long run, it is better to pay the tolls along the road to success now than leave them for your child to pay later.

Do I have any entitlement to my child's earnings?

The short answer to this question is this: very little, if any. If you are entitled to anything, it will come in one of two forms: reimbursement for expenses or compensation for services rendered. There are unique financial and legal hurdles to each situation, however, that must be cleared for you to be entitled to anything. First, any compensation you will receive must be tied to a service you will provide for the child and be outlined in detail in a contract. If you are to be the child's manager, a specific arrangement including services and payment must be contained in the contract. Simply being a parent (even a wonderful and supportive one) does not entitle you to a portion of your child's earnings.

Facilitating your child's career will undoubtedly entail numerous expenses that you will have to pay out. You may seek to be reimbursed for these costs from your child's income, but such reimbursements are not without limits. Accountant and business manager Harvey Tanton notes that some of the things you cannot be reimbursed for include living expenses for living in your own home, meals at home, and lessons your child received prior to the time when you and your child entered a formal agreement about your management of his or her career.[17] Harvey advises parents to separate out any such expenses that any parent would normally incur when raising a child from those extra expenses that are incurred exclusively because your child is pursuing a career in performance. He also recommends that parents set a clear start date for reimbursements, noting it in writing, so that the money can be repaid to them for the costs of lessons, travel, and so forth after that date.

Understand that undertaking the task of pursuing a show business career for your child is no inexpensive matter. You, as parent, will most likely see little monetary return on investment, save for the limited situations above, but will be rewarded by the joy your child finds in his or her successful career.

What expenses can I claim on my taxes?

Taxes can be the most difficult toll to pay on this journey because you have expenses that will pile up, and it can be tempting to simply pay them without thinking of the consequences. As a parent, you have a fiduciary relationship with your child: you must do what is in the best interests of the child, not yourself. It is imperative that you reserve enough money to pay the taxes on what your child earns each year. As mentioned above, the best way to ensure that this happens is to find a qualified professional, such as an accountant or business manager, to handle tax matters. If you can, find an accountant with prior experience in accounting in the entertainment field. This will help you deal with the industry-specific tax implications of your child's chosen profession and ensure that your financial advisor understands the nuances of any business entities you may form to handle your child's income. If you choose to handle your taxes yourself, be careful, as things can spiral out of control very quickly. Barry Klarberg clarifies that pursuant to the Internal Revenue Code, normal and legitimate business expenses are deductible, including business meals. Expenses used to maintain your child's profession, such as hiring a voice coach, are only deductible to the extent that your child already has an established career and are not being paid for in pursuit of a "new career." Conversely, expenses used to give your child initial vocal training before the child has established a career are not deductible.

"Loan Out" Entities

Another way in which to help deal with the sometimes daunting tax implications is to create a business entity in order to be able to write off a greater number of expenses, often known as a "loan out" entity. A "loan out" entity is precisely what it sounds like: it is a business organization that you create, of which your child is an employee, which "loans out" your child to those seeking his or her services. The general rule is that if your child is consistently earning an excess of $100,000 per year, it is worthwhile to open up a "loan out" entity. This is not a hard and fast rule, however, so be sure to review this with your accountant to ensure that doing so would be the right move for you and your child. It is important to make certain that your child is consistently earning the above sum before you form the entity.

Accountants and business managers can recommend what type of "loan out" entity makes the most sense for your child's career and, depending on the situation, some professionals may differ in opinion. For example, accountant and business manager Harvey Tanton recommends setting up a separate single-member limited liability company (LLC) to prevent commingling funds with your child's finances, obtain legal protection, and achieve disregarded status for tax purposes. Accountant and business manager Errol Wander, on the other hand, favors corporations for single performers because LLCs are more likely to get audited in situations where the entity has $100,000 in revenues coupled with $80,000 in expenses. The particular "loan out" entity you form for your child's career will also be required by the IRS to pay "reasonable and regular" salaries to employees. Errol Wander further recommends obtaining appropriate levels of insurance for the entity, including unemployment and worker's compensation, when you hire a touring crew to assist your young artist on the road to avoid liability.

Finally, if and when you form a "loan out" entity, you must ensure that it is run like a real business. Someone must run the company and keep proper records, be that a business manager or yourself. This means that that person must keep proper records of revenues, expenses, taxes, and so forth. You could choose to be an officer of the corporation or to have other people fill the roles of corporate officers. Certain officers would have the power to assign your child's rights that are vested in the corporation, such as right of publicity, trademark, and copyrights, so make sure you thoroughly discuss any choices you are going to make with your management team. As an officer of the corporation, you may be permitted to draw a salary, but it cannot be excessive. Again, you must ensure that everything is done legitimately and take your role as an officer seriously. This is a situation in which you must separate yourself from your role as "parent" and embrace your role as "business partner." Do not make the mistake of viewing this position as a way to siphon some of your child's earnings to pay personal expenses. The IRS will want to see that the corporation is being run as it should and is not simply serving to reduce tax liability.

The differing but equally valuable viewpoints within the financial services industry show parents just how important it is to obtain second opinions and determine exactly what financial arrangement and professional representation is best for their child. Remember, in the end, financial planning is not a one-size-fits-all model and must be tailored to best serve the individual needs of you and your child.

CHAPTER 5

Maintenance and Repairs

How can I protect my child's health and happiness?

EVEN THE MOST FINELY TUNED and reliable machine will break down with enough wear and tear. Regardless of whether your child may be the human equivalent of a Volvo, the stress of maintaining a professional life *and* personal life can be personally hazardous. This strain can place your child's physical and mental health in jeopardy, and it will fall upon you to keep them safe. A career in entertainment, especially a burgeoning one, can be seductive. It is easy to forget that there are responsibilities and basic needs that your child has outside of the career. But a constant focus on career and not the long-term mental and emotional health of your child can lead to a breakdown. If your child is pushed too quickly in any one direction, he or she may neglect the other aspects of life, and this could lead to very serious short- and long-term consequences. Balance is, more than anything, what will keep your child on the road to being a successful person, not merely a successful entertainer.

No matter how talented your child is, it is imperative that he or she has a life outside of the entertainment world. The temptation to let your child slip entirely into his or her professional life might arise, but it is your job to ensure that this does not happen. You, too, must be vigilant of your own risk of becoming so focused on your child's career that you forget about all other aspects of your child's and your own life. By becoming so focused on pursuing your child's entertainment career, you may end up pushing your child too hard and exponentially increasing your child's risk of "burning out." Accountant and business manager Errol Wander recalls a client who wanted to put her six-year-old piano prodigy child on a tour bus. In doing so, that parent would be isolating the child from all other aspects of his or her young life. Secluded on a tour bus, the child would eat, sleep, and breathe his or her career, and nothing more. In Errol's opinion, if a child excels at music at such a young age, locking him or her into a music and entertainment career may preclude options of pursuing another honorable career path and potentially stunt his or her social and emotional growth in other areas.

One way to keep your child's life well rounded is to keep your child in mainstream schools as much as possible as he or she pursues a career in show business. There are two major benefits that flow from keeping your child in school. First, creative artists draw on their life experiences to create material. It fuels their performances so that they can better connect with their audience. Exposing your child to a range of people with diverse interests during his or her formative years will enrich his or her life experience. Keeping your child with other children who are not a part of the industry will keep his or her grounded and connected to mainstream society. Moreover, the theater and music programs at normal schools place your child in creative programs with non-entertainment-oriented children. Exposing your child to others who are involved in the arts, not for the hope of monetary gain but for the sheer joy of participating, will pay dividends in the long run by combating burnout and fatigue, hopefully reminding your child why she or he began pursuing a show business career in the first place.

A second, and possibly more important, benefit to keeping your child in school is that even if your child has the talent to succeed in the industry, he or she may tire of the life that success requires. The simple fact is that most people who go into creative arts will not make it. Your child deserves a safety net in case he or she decides ultimately not to pursue a career in the arts. It is unhealthy to have his or her life revolve around one thing, no matter how attractive that "thing" may seem.

How can I make sure my child still focuses on schoolwork while pursuing a career?

Your child may tell you that he or she loves performing and can handle schoolwork as well as a career, but if reality tells a different tale, you must be responsible enough to put your child's future first and alter its course or shut down the career. Letting your child know that the career is only available if he or she completes their schoolwork will serve as strong motivation to keep them focused on school.

A career in the arts at such a young age entails a tremendous amount of sacrifice. The career will be a major time investment. Vital to your child's ability to balance school and work will be your ability to manage your child's schedule. This means creating a schedule that allows adequate time for both career and schoolwork. Your child's life must be highly organized. Weekends will almost certainly be used to catch up on schoolwork for the week. Learn to be efficient with your child's time as well. This does not, however, mean cutting corners to fit in more. It means that in your child's life, time is a scarce resource that you control, and you cannot afford to waste any of it. It will be difficult, and in the end, you and your child may well decide that the sacrifice required is not justified by the reward. But if your child believes strongly in moving forward with his or her career, you must find a way to be efficient and regimented to ensure that your child's education does not suffer.

There are many times where your child's career may require him or her to travel and be away from school for an extended period of time. As mentioned before, it is important (and sometimes legally mandatory) to hire an on-site tutor to ensure your child keeps up on his studies and does not fall behind his class. For the Arciero Sisters, Jillian, Olivia, Dominique, and Gabriela, touring with their country music band took them on the road for weeks at a time. To ensure the girls were still getting the education they needed, their parents took school lessons into their own hands and created a unique curriculum that was compatible with their on-the-road lifestyle. To name a few aspects, their approach featured instructional software specially tailored for each daughter's grade level (which the girls viewed on their laptops while traveling), independent study of topics of the daughters' choice, and educational field trips to businesses, museums, and famous landmarks. Susan even had the girls listen to French language tapes during rides from gig to gig.[18]

Like the Arciero sisters, former child actor Lara Jill Miller did not have the traditional schooling experience. Instead of spending her days in middle school and high school, she worked with on-site tutors while filming the popular 1980s NBC sitcom, *Gimme A Break*. In Lara's case, after *Gimme A Break* ended, she enjoyed a traditional college experience by enrolling in New York University. After experiencing academic success as an undergraduate, Lara obtained her law degree at Fordham University and enjoyed professional success practicing as an attorney in New York City. Upon practicing law for two years, Lara returned to show business as a voice-over actress celebrated in children's shows such as *Curious George*, *SciGirls*, *Rugrats*, *Clifford's Puppy Days*, *Wow Wow Wubbzy*, and *Doc McStuffins*, among many others. Lara's story demonstrates that child actors can enjoy success in college, graduate school, and beyond. However, knowing that having a career in show business as a child does not always carry through into adulthood, Lara made the prudent decision to secure an alternative, mainstream career path in case she found herself unable to succeed in returning to show business as an adult.

How can I raise my child as a "good person" and not just a "good performer?"

In a word: balance. It is a simple concept but a very difficult one to implement and master. Keeping your child grounded and maintaining balance in his or her life will take care of making your child a good person. But what defines a good person? There is no accepted standard definition of a "good person," so what you should instead focus on is getting your child to make responsible, well-founded choices.

Making positive choices flows from having good judgment, and good judgment is learned in the real world—not the narrow world of professional performers. Though others may disagree, there are sound reasons to place your child in a special performing arts school. My wife and I chose otherwise. We believe that there are far more compelling reasons not to do so. One of the main reasons is the exposure to others with diverse interests, and fostering diverse interests in your child helps build character and promote good judgment. Another way is to keep your child involved in family and friend activities whenever possible. If you have standard family activities in place, such as game nights or family dinners, you will keep your child involved. Furthermore, expose your child to positive role models outside of the performance arena. Expand your child's knowledge of how others not in the industry conduct themselves, so that they may expand their worldview.

Philanthropy

Another way to maintain balance and build character is to require your child to participate in philanthropy. This goes beyond merely donating earnings to charity, which will have almost no impact on character. Instead, have them work at a hospital, a soup kitchen, or anywhere they can help others to experience first-hand the fruits of their efforts. Making a hands-on effort provides a dual benefit. Your child will be exposed to an aspect of life they may otherwise never have seen, and it will help to instill a sense that there is more to life than money or fame. Not only will your child truly see and understand the benefits of helping others, but to interact with others who may be less fortunate will be a truly humbling experience. Your child will spend a considerable amount of time around people and other children who are impressed with his or her success. Requiring your child to perform charity work will go a long way in the battle to keep his or her head out of the clouds and feet on the ground.

CHAPTER 6

Taking the Wheel

How can I manage the business of my child's career while still being his or her parent?

IN THE MIDST OF THE excitement and chaos of developing their child's career, some parents lose track of their primary duty: to be a *parent*. Throughout the process, your child will look to you for encouragement and support as well as for praise for a job well done. In the words of Eileen DeNobile, "Parental support to professional children comes in the form of encouragement, cooperation, and the ability to drive to auditions. In order for the parent and child to succeed as a team, the parent must be cooperative in providing support, and the child needs to be appreciative of the support he or she is receiving from Mom or Dad."

Though such encouragement is necessary, your child will also need constant guidance and discipline to keep him or her grounded and focused. Just because your child has achieved a certain status in his or her career does not make your child immune to punishment and taking responsibility for misbehaviors. You must remove your "star-studded glasses" and recognize that it is still your job as parent to keep your child in line. Remind your child that, no matter the level of his or her success, he or she is still *your child* and must abide by your rules and behave according to the morals and values you've instilled in them.

That said, it is also important to have a business-minded approach to advancing your child's career. When dealing in the "business" of your child's career, always remember that it is your *child's* interests that you are advancing, *not* your own. Business decisions regarding your child's show business career should be based upon his or her desires and not solely upon the direction that *you* think his or her career should take. Remember, however, that your child is, in fact, just a child. Just as in any other aspect of your child's life, you must invoke your parental authority and impose your "better judgment" over that of your child's in order to protect and guide them.

Balance Your Parental View

There may be times when your child wants to jump at certain business opportunities or jobs that, according to your informed judgment, are inappropriate or not good "business moves" for your child's career. As a parent and "business partner," you must always advise your child against or even prevent him or her from making certain moves or decisions that could be harmful to your child or your child's career. It is important, however, not to become too restricting or overbearing in the business aspect. Although you are a "parent first," don't let your instinctive over-protection cloud your business judgment. Let your "parental view" and your "business view" be a check on each other. A helpful way of maintaining this delicate balance is to perform a self-check every so often. You can also seek the opinion of a third party to ensure that you are adequately dealing with your child's career while still being the best parent you can be.

How can I employ effective business tactics while still being a good role model for my child?

The business world is known for cutthroat tactics and hard-nosed deal negotiations. This is especially true in the competitive field of entertainment. Along the road to your child's success, you may be faced with situations where it will take a lot of force and argument to get what you and your child want from a business deal or job. You may find yourself acting in a manner in which you would normally not conduct yourself and would definitely not want your child to mirror. When faced with such a difficult situation, remember that your child still looks to you as a role model. Your child will internalize what he or she sees you doing and saying and conclude that that is the appropriate way to act. To ensure that you do not inadvertently teach your child these "wicked ways" of the business world, speak with your child about the importance of respect when dealing with others. Being expressly told of the "appropriate" way to conduct business will make it clear to your child the type of behavior that is expected of him or her.

As a parent, however, you cannot raise your child in show business solely on the motto of "do as I say, not as I do." It is important that you, too, follow your own advice on appropriate business conduct and remember to treat others with respect, no matter how difficult or argumentative they may be. There may be a time when a person you are dealing with will be extremely uncooperative. Stand your ground, with authority and class, and show your child how to fight for what's right and how to fight the "right way." If it is not too much against your child's best interest, it may be a smart move to know when to compromise. This business move in itself will be a lesson to your child in cooperation. Explain to your child the importance of give-and-take in some situations, and emphasize that compromise is *not* defeat, but a success in itself.

Another key business lesson you can teach your child is the importance of honoring your own agreement. Once you and another party reach an agreement, make sure to fulfill your end of the bargain. This will show your child the importance of honoring his or her own. For example, your child will learn that if he or she agrees to do a photo shoot at a certain date and time, he or she cannot simply decide, "I don't want to go to that photo shoot, so I'm not going." Let your child know that there are *two* sides and many people involved in any agreement, and by not honoring his or her responsibilities, those other people are being let down and inconvenienced. Inform your child that in addition to making others "feel bad" by not upholding a commitment, he or she will be creating a bad reputation for him- or herself, which will affect how and if other people want to work with your child in the future.

As a last resort, if it is inevitable to avoid conflict in business dealings regarding your child's career, make sure never to engage in disrespectful or unsavory behavior in your child's presence. Take care to do so in a place where your child will not hear or see your actions and thus learn by example. If you sense a situation getting heated, and your child is present, take a moment to regain your composure, and either ask your child to "wait outside" out of earshot, or remove yourself from the situation entirely, postponing the negotiations until a later time.

Remember, no matter how "into" your business role in your child's career you are, you are still your child's parent. He or she looks up to you as a role model and will inevitably learn and mimic your behaviors. By discussing the proper ways to conduct business with your child, and acting appropriately yourself, you can set a good example and raise a respectful and business-savvy child.

How much is "too much" involvement in the business of my child's show business career?

We've all heard the horror stories about "stage parents" who control their children and micro-manage their careers. You probably look at those parents and think to yourself, "I'll never be like that!" Unfortunately, that's probably the same attitude those parents you criticize started out with. You can, however, take measures to ensure that you do not fall into the same dangerous course of conduct as they have. By keeping an eye open for certain warning signs, and periodically doing a "red flag" check, you can keep yourself in line.

Don't Interfere

One sign that it is time to pull back is when your involvement begins to interfere with the ability of other professionals involved in your child's career to do their job. Directors, producers, instructors, and agents cannot carry out their responsibilities if you constantly interfere with their efficiency and question their judgment. Music Producer Jimmy Landry has worked with several artists under the age of eighteen, and only a couple of the parents adequately understood what it means to be a cooperative professional parent. Jimmy explains that creative professionals and parents are interdependent. Parents should provide support and assist the creative professionals by motivating their children, relieving the pressure, and lightening their children's load. This can be achieved by such small efforts as staying in the same building as the studio where the child is undergoing a recording session and checking in every forty-five minutes or so. Jimmy elaborates that parents who did not fully understand their role micro-managed or otherwise behaved like the stereotypical "stage parent," making the job of the professionals more difficult.

Although you should always keep a watchful eye for outright misconduct, matters of professional judgment should be left to . . . well . . . the professionals. Remember, the director or producer is essentially "the boss," and your child is the employee. *You* are simply an advisor and facilitator. In the case of a manager and an agent, you hired them for a reason. You were impressed by their skill and felt comfortable putting your child's career in their hands. You therefore need to place your trust in them and let them do the job you hired them to do.

Don't Overcommit

A second "red flag" of too much involvement arises when you begin to neglect your other personal duties for the sake of your child's career. Frequent absences from work or lack of productivity may prompt employer disappointment. Failing to pay attention to the other relationships in your life, be they children, spouse, family, or friends, may lead to complaints and feelings of neglect and abandonment. If any such situations are brought to your attention, it is time for you to reconsider how much involvement you have in your child's career.

Remember that your child and his or her career are merely one aspect of your life, not the be-all-and-end-all of your existence. In order to maintain a healthy perspective on your and your child's lives, you cannot devote all of your energy to ensuring your child achieves success in show business. Your child's happiness is contingent upon your own happiness because it dictates how you will conduct yourself toward your child, toward others, and in the course of your child's career. This means prioritizing. You, too, have a life. You have a family, a job, a home, friends, all of which need attention and nurturing and to which you have responsibilities as well. As we will address in following chapters, neglecting any of these areas will undoubtedly lead to resentment on both ends and, in a "worst case scenario" a loss of employment and thus loss of income that would severely hinder your child's career path.

Loosen the Pressure

Finally, a third major sign that you are on the path to becoming an overbearing "stage parent" is your child's unhappiness. When your child begins to exhibit signs that he or she is unhappy and no longer enjoys performing, it may be a result of your constant pressure. Your child's lack of interest may arise from the fact that he or she is no longer pursuing his or her dream but, rather, yours. Former agent Halle Madia, manager Eileen DeNobile, and casting directors Beth Melsky and Adrienne Stern have all cited the prevalence of children they encounter who have absolutely no interest in pursuing a career in the entertainment industry, but are merely doing so to appease their parents. If you sense your child's hesitation or lack of interest, sit them down and talk to them about the source of their reactions. Encourage them to be honest with you about how they feel about the way their career path is going and if they want to keep pursuing it. If it is something you are doing that is making show business not enjoyable for your child, you know it is time to take a step back and let your child "do his or her thing." Children have a talent for being brutally honest, so take whatever your child has to say to heart, or you may end up bringing about the end of your child's entertainment career.

It is not always easy to spot these warning signs yourself, so it is helpful to seek the opinions of others. Consult your spouse, other children, family members, and friends. Ask them to keep an eye out for these signs as well and to confront you about them if they sense there is a problem. This way, you can prevent yourself from developing a nasty case of "stage parent" syndrome and keep yourself, your child, and everyone else in your life satisfied and happy.

How can I maintain an unbiased perspective of my child, his or her talent, and career?

Over the course of your child's career, it is easy for you to become so involved that you come to believe that your child can do no wrong, is perfect for every role, and deserves every "perk" known to man. This is especially so given that parents have an innate pride in their child and are thus inherently biased when assessing their talents and performance. As mentioned earlier, it is important that you maintain an outsider's view of your child's talents. Periodically reassess your child's abilities and the direction in which his or her career is headed. Continue to seek outside and expert opinion, and welcome any critiques others may have. Consider your child's professional progress. Is your child getting roles or gigs on a regular basis? Are they substantial? Continue to compare your child to other "successful" child stars within the industry. How does your child's progress and skill compare to others in his or her age group, skill set, and field? By asking yourself these questions, and taking on the "eyes" of an outsider, you can avoid becoming overly biased about your child's abilities. Remember, however, not to confuse "bias" with pride in your child. No matter how you answer the above questions, always reassure your child that you are proud of him or her and that you have faith in your child. Knowing you are proud of him or her will undoubtedly be motivation for your child to work and practice harder to improve his or her talents even more.

What do I do when what is best for my child conflicts with what is best for my child's career?

Your child's physical and emotional well-being are paramount. There may come a time where a course of action requires something of your child that puts that well-being at risk but may advance your child's career. For example, perhaps your child has been booked for several big musical performances within a short period of time. This breach will undoubtedly provide considerable exposure and lead to additional opportunities. However, the intensity of the performance, combined with a rigorous travel schedule, may leave your child physically exhausted, sleep-deprived, and emotionally drained. What should you do?

Another example is if your child lands a principal role in a horror movie where your child will be exposed to stage blood and violence. Do you allow your child to take on the role and advance his or her career? Casting director Adrienne Stern points out that professional children are often forced to grow up much more quickly than their peers, which may be a concern for you as a parent. Professional child actors spend most of their time with adults during lessons and during filming. Moreover, often times the material being filmed contains adult content such as sex or horror. As a parent you must evaluate whether your child's career in the entertainment business is worth these potential side effects.

No matter the appeal of what could be your child's "big break," it is never worth sacrificing your child's health and happiness. If such a conflict of interests is easily avoidable, avoid it. For example, if the above situations were not a potential "big break" and would not have a substantial impact on your child's career, there is no need to pursue the opportunity or take that specific path to "success." If the opportunity *would* provide a significant advantage to your child's career, find a way to counteract or eliminate the conflict. Bring your concerns to the attention of the person who wishes to hire your child, be it a producer, director, or whomever, and ask how he or she can accommodate your child such that no harm will come to him or her. This may take a bit of persuasion or negotiation if what that person requires of your child is essential to his or her "vision"; however, if the job is really worth it, some arrangement can and must be met. Any person worth working for will not want to put your child's well-being at risk.

If a situation ever arises in which the next step in your child's career would be a detriment to what is best for your child, and that conflict cannot be avoided, then something, somewhere, went wrong. It is time to get out. No career is worth sacrificing the well-being of your child, and his or her health, happiness, and safety must be placed above all else.

What are the reasonable sacrifices my child will be required to make in pursuing his or her career?

As much fun as your child's pursuit of a career in entertainment may be, the road to success will not be an easy Sunday drive. Your child will have to make some sacrifices in exchange for the greater goal of pursuing his or her dream of a career in show business. After all, not only does your child have the typical responsibilities of a child his or her age, but he or she also has the added responsibilities of maintaining a career, a set of responsibilities usually reserved for "grown-ups." Thus, one sacrifice your child will have to make is to become a bit more mature more quickly than his or her peers. The business of show business requires professionalism and practice and carries with it many obligations. Your child will need to quickly learn how to manage all of the above as a "little adult." However, it is up to you, as his or her parent, to make sure your child does not grow up *too* fast or *too* much such that he or she never really gets to be "just a kid." You must use your best judgment to ensure that that fine line is not crossed.

Less "Free Time"

The added responsibilities of a career in show business will result in a much busier schedule than the average child would encounter. This leaves your children with less opportunity for "down time" and recreational activities. Play dates with friends will be fewer and farther between, and watching Saturday morning cartoons every weekend may become a nonentity. This is one reason why it is crucial to make sure your child truly enjoys what he or she is doing in his or her career so that your child will actually consider activities related thereto as "recreation" and fun. As much as the frequency of such "down time" activities will decrease, it is important to ensure that they are not eliminated from your child's schedule altogether. Children, whether they are "stars in the making" or "just regular kids," need to play and relax in order to grow, learn, and be happy. Parent Tess Filsoof describes her daughter Rachel's friends as wonderful people who contribute to her balanced life, which also includes school, family, performance coaching, auditions, and filming her latest movies. Like Tess, be sure to infuse your child's daily grind of school, lessons, rehearsals, tapings, and performances with some opportunities for good-old-fashioned fun.

Jealousy

In your son's or daughter's attempts to maintain a sense of childhood normalcy, he or she may unfortunately encounter envious peers whose jealousy will make them treat your child poorly and try to put him or her down. Children often resort to cruelty such as teasing or bullying when they let the "green-eyed monster" take over. Even former friends may begin to treat your child differently than before he or she began to pursue a career in show business. This change in the attitudes of others may result in your child feeling as if he or she did something "wrong" to make people not like him or her. Your child may cite his or her career as the source of the animosity, thus cooling his or her desire to pursue that path. Furthermore, his or her self-esteem may suffer, or he or she may begin to "act out" or partake in activities he or she would otherwise not entertain, in order to try to reenter their good graces.

It is important that you quash any such thoughts of fault immediately. Reassure your child that the way his or her peers are acting toward him or her is not due to any malfeasance on your child's part but rather the result of the envious feelings of the other children. Tell your child that his or her peers recognize the wonderful opportunity he or she has been given and wish they could be blessed with the same. Emphasize that these children are still the same good-hearted people your child knew before, but they simply let their emotions get the best of them. Sooner or later, they will come around, and those who are truly your child's friends will learn to accept your child's career choice and become genuinely supportive of him or her. In the unfortunate case your child ends up permanently losing a formerly good friend, use the occasion as an opportunity to talk to your child about feelings and the different roles people play in our lives, whether they are in them forever or for only a short time. Highlight the importance of forgiveness, and encourage your child not to bear any resentment or ill will toward the abandoning friend. It may be difficult for your child at first, but in the game of show business, one filled with rejection and transient players, the earlier your child learns to cope with such occurrences with grace, the better equipped and happier he or she will be throughout his or her career.

Health Comes First

One thing your child should not be required to sacrifice is his or her health. The daily stresses and responsibilities of the career pursuit will lead to endless days on the road and schedules jam-packed with appearances, auditions, and performances. All of this activity may take a toll on your child's mental and physical health. It is thus important to schedule your child's doctor, dentist, and other health-related appointments as often as, if not more than, usual. Your child is your most precious gift, and making sure he or she is kept in good physical, mental, and emotional health is your most important responsibility as a parent. No amount of show business success is worth sacrificing your child's health and happiness.

CHAPTER 7

Protecting the Other Passengers

What kinds of sacrifices will I be required to make in facilitating my child's career?

YOU, AS A PARENT, ARE a crucial part of your child's success. You, ever protective, are there ensuring that your child stays on the road. On top of this responsibility, however, you have an added challenge: to make sure your life stays the course as well. Few people can afford to spend all day in the car with no other responsibilities to concern themselves with. In fact, it may be impossible to manage your own career, your child's career, and your family life all at once. Only you will know what you can or cannot handle. It will fall to you to figure out what can stay in your life and what can be sacrificed to keep your child's dreams alive.

Pursuing a career in show business is a time-consuming task for both you and your child. Devoting your efforts to this feat will result in less time to devote to other aspects of your life, such as your own career, social life, and even the other members of your family.

Relocating

You and your family will be faced with some important decisions, such as whether to relocate to entertainment hubs such as New York or Los Angeles in order to have easier access to auditions. Casting director Beth Melsky explains that if you want to work in New York, you must be within traveling distance, which is two hours or less even in traffic. Therefore, even Philadelphia can be too far away. Professional parents

Tess Filsoof and Susan Jones both reflect that relocating to New York contributed to their children's success. Child actor Lara Jill Miller notes that if her mother had been unwilling to relocate to Los Angeles, she would not have been able to star in *Gimme A Break* and achieve the same level of professional success as a child. Manager Eileen DeNobile notes, however, that although moving to New York or Los Angeles may make it easier to audition, there is no guarantee on how many auditions you will secure or that you will book legitimate work. This sound advice should be considered before uprooting your family because of your child's career aspirations.

Time with Other Family Members

Perhaps the most difficult of the sacrifices you will make as a professional parent to accept is the diminishing time you will have to spend with your spouse, other children, and the rest of your family. Because your attention will be mainly fixated on your show business child, you run the risk of alienating the rest of your family. Pursuing your child's career may require you to be separated from your spouse and other children for extended periods of time, which will challenge your relationships with them. In order to avoid alienation and preserve and nurture your relationships with the other members of your family, it is imperative that you maintain open, honest, and supportive lines of communication. Always keep them informed and updated on your efforts and enthusiastically acknowledge all of their talents and interests as well. Whenever possible, make a conscious effort to attend the activities of your non-show-business children and do so with zeal and excitement. Attend baseball games and piano recitals. Keep abreast of your children's schoolwork, and remain informed about their personal and social lives. Do not lose sight of what is truly important: the integrity of your family. It is crucial that each and every member of your family understands and feels that they are important to and loved by you each in their own individual way. No parent wants to sacrifice the affection of one child for the "stardom" of another.

Your spouse or partner can be your greatest ally in maintaining this delicate balance. He or she will help keep you involved in all of your children's lives and provide a "reality check" if that balancing act begins to go awry. Let your spouse know that every so often, when the pursuit of your child's career becomes overwhelming, you will need a gentle reminder of what is truly important. That said, your relationship with your spouse is the other vital relationship you cannot sacrifice in your child's career quest. It, too, must be nurtured to foster the united parental front necessary for a happy family. Not only will the teamwork between the two of you ensure a healthy and orderly home environment, but it will ensure personal happiness as well. Make sure your spouse knows how much you appreciate all that he or she does and all of the extra responsibilities he or she picks up while you are focusing on your child in show business. Take the time to plan "date nights" on days when you are both at home. Enlist the help of another family member or a trusted babysitter and plan a rendezvous if you are on the road with your child and away from each other for a while. Even a constant stream of affectionate emails or notes can keep the flame alive. Whatever you do, make sure it is clear that your spouse is an important and valued part of your life that you rely on and could not live without. Happy parents will make for a happy, cohesive family that should not be sacrificed for a career in show business.

Relationship with Your Child

Your relationship with your show business child will change as well. Although you are, as emphasized throughout this book, first and foremost your child's parent, there is an added element of a business-like relationship. The professional aspect of your role in helping your child achieve his or her dream of show business success will often put a strain on the dynamic of your relationship. You will no longer be your child's "best friend" at all times, as you will often be encouraging your child to do things he or she does not "feel like" doing because you know that such things will be beneficial to your child and/or to your child's career. Viewing your child/parent relationship through this professional lens may lead to tension between the two of you. Much like other aspects of parenting in general, however, you must recognize that what you are encouraging or discouraging your child to do or not do is ultimately for his or her benefit, and sooner or later he or she will recognize this. You will not be the "bad guy" forever. If your relationship begins to get too resentful or tense, it may be time to reevaluate your role in your child's career pursuit.

Finances

In addition to personal career sacrifices, discussed in the next chapter, you will have to make financial sacrifices when helping your child pursue his or her career. Pursuing a career in show business is by no means inexpensive. Coaches, professional photographs, airfare, and lodging are just some of the numerous expenses you will incur in your child's journey to show business success. As mentioned earlier, it is important to maintain proper business records and a budget throughout the entire process. In time, your child's career will help to finance itself. Before this point, and perhaps to some extent even after, you and your family will have less of a surplus of funds to spend on miscellaneous indulgent expenses such as, for example, dinners out, expensive clothing, or exotic vacations. Careful budgeting and some sacrifice of usual luxuries may be required to keep your family's finances in check.

Social Life

Finally, but by no means least importantly, your own social life may suffer as a result of your involvement in your child's quest for stardom. Just as you will have less time to devote to your family and your career, so will you have less time to spend with your friends and on activities you personally enjoy. A lack of contact with friends may lead to strained relationships and feelings of alienation. Like every relationship, friendship requires attention and nurturing in order to thrive. Be sure to keep your friends in the know about your and your child's activities, and, likewise, keep informed about your friends' lives. It may be helpful to agree to send weekly emails to each other just to "catch up," extol your highs of the week, and lament your lows. Friends offer us an honest view of ourselves, as well as an escape from the stresses of our daily family lives. Do not lose these relationships. They will be a great source of support as you work with your child on his or her career.

No matter how consuming your child's career pursuit may become, you must always remember that it is neither selfish nor irresponsible to take some time to focus on yourself. A night out with friends, dinner and a movie with your spouse, or simply a quiet moment reading a book and soaking in the tub may provide you with the stress release you need to maintain your own happiness and a balanced life. A happy, rejuvenated you will be more beneficial to your child, family, and those around you, and you will be much better equipped to help attack your child's career pursuit head-on with gusto.

Is it possible to manage my own career while facilitating my child's?

Nothing is impossible, but it can be stunningly difficult to reconcile a full-time livelihood with your child's career. With all of the time spent focusing on your child's career, you will inevitably have less time to devote to a career of your own. Most careers cannot accommodate the need for you to fly off for a few days to take your child on an audition across the country or accompany your child as he or she is on a movie set for days, weeks, or months. This is not to say that maintaining your own career is impossible. To do so, however, will require a heightened level of organization and prioritization as well as added help from family members. It is also helpful to discuss options and possible accommodations with your superiors at work. Many may be sympathetic to your needs and find some way to enable you to maintain your own career while you help your child pursue his or hers.

The most ideal way to handle your child's career is, if you are married, to have one spouse handle their own career while the other handles the child's. If this is impossible, you will need to enlist other family members to help you. There are only twenty-four hours in each day, and spending eight to twelve of those hours on your own career leaves little time for your child's. The requirements of a child star's profession are simply not conducive to reasonably maintaining a full-time career of your own. If you do have a full-time career that you cannot be away from, there is no harm in seeking out other responsible adult family members to be with your child throughout all of this. A child is woefully ill-equipped to handle the rigors of a professional schedule on his or her own. What is important is that you find someone whom you trust, whom your child trusts, and who is capable of stepping in to fill what would normally be your day-to-day role in your child's career.

How can I balance my home life and my child's career?

Even if you do not have a career of your own to attend to, you may have other familial responsibilities that you cannot abandon to pursue your child's career. If possible, occasionally have another family member chaperone your child on auditions or on set. This will free up time for you to maintain your obligations to the rest of your family. If you do not have another family member who can do this, you will have to become a master scheduler and planner.

Learn to multi-task to free up the time you need to attend to both the child's career and the rest of your family. This is especially important if you have other children who are not in the business. Failing to maintain your relationship and obligations to them in favor of your other child's show business career will lead to neglect, bitterness, jealousy, and ultimately resentment. One way in which you can demonstrate to your children that there is no favoritism is by maintaining normal family requirements for all of your children. If each child has chores, do not let your child off the hook for them because he or she was working. Participation in an entertainment career is a choice; if he or she cannot handle the career and the family requirements, he or she should not be allowed to continue. Letting your child know that he or she still has family responsibilities will keep him or her grounded and let the other children know that you are not favoring that child because of his or her career.

Susan Jones took a different, though no less effective, approach to combating sibling jealousy. When her daughter Jillian was cast on Broadway, her other daughters felt excluded, and it created a division among her daughters. In an effort to make all of her daughters feel equally important, Susan made the executive decision as a parent to have all three work together to form the country music girl band, the Little Women Band. By having them all involved in show business, Susan was able to ensure that they all felt equally included and grew even closer as a family through the experience.

Will the rest of my family's lifestyle change?

The short answer to this question is "absolutely." Your family will notice a change in their own daily lives due to your child's pursuit of his or her show business career and your involvement with it. Your family will have less time with you and less time with your show business child as the two of you wage the crusade for success in whatever area of show business your child is involved. They may find themselves having to vie for your attention and sacrifice their own interests for the sake of your show business child's schedule. Though you may try to enlist the involvement of your other family members in your child's career quest in hopes that such cooperation will foster family unity, they may find such an assignment to be mundane and insulting, as if you feel the whole family should revolve around your show business child. Your other children may begin to act out in hopes of gleaning whatever attention they can from you or as a way of expressing their jealousy and resentment of their show business brother or sister. Thus, when asking or suggesting involvement in your child's career, approach such a topic delicately, and make sure you are not forcing them to take part. If they agree to participate in some way, make sure you do not over-involve them and run the risk of using your family as if they are "just another member of your child's show business team." They are, in fact, your family, and they play a greater role in your life than that of "assistant."

As previously mentioned, your family may notice there are fewer surplus funds to pay for the little indulgences they may have enjoyed prior to your child's involvement in show business. On the other hand, once your child's career becomes lucrative, the family may find themselves with *more* money than they are used to having at their disposal. This, too, can be a major change that may take some getting used to and will require discipline to properly manage, but it can be a slight silver lining to offset or prevent some of the other sacrifices that must be made. Remember, however, that money alone does not a happy family make.

Keep Traditions Alive

To prevent your family's lifestyle from too much change and sacrifice, it is important to maintain some normalcy by holding true to the traditions your family shared before your child began pursuing a career in show business. Plan the family vacations you look forward to every year. Have those Wednesday night family dinners that allow everyone to catch up on each others' lives. Show that the pillars that provide stability for your family are still firmly in place. Your family will appreciate the comfort of familiar plans and schedules during this hectic time when your child's show business pursuits may require you to be anywhere at any time.

If your and your child's schedules cannot accommodate these old family traditions, create new ones. For example, if you can no longer have Wednesday night dinners due to travel schedule or voice lessons, institute a Monday family game night or Sunday morning brunch instead. Though not a "tradition" per se, adding a pet to the family may foster a sense of unity and responsibility and add an element of excitement and comfort. Whatever the new tradition may be, your family will appreciate the effort you make to maintain some consistency in their lifestyles, which will in turn allow them to adjust more easily to any changes they may encounter as a result of your child's show business career.

Don't Be Blinded by the Spotlight

Another change your family may experience is an increase in public exposure. Once your child achieves a certain level of fame in his or her career, your family's privacy may suffer. They may be placed under greater media and public scrutiny and lose their protective shield of anonymity. Furthermore, they risk losing their individual identities as they may come to be known as "so-and-so's brother, sister, father, or mother." There are two key points to emphasize herein. First, address the issue of increased public scrutiny with your family. Encourage them to continue living their lives as they always have. Alert them, however, of the added importance of being mindful of how they conduct themselves in their private lives, as it very well may be made public. Second, if you sense any family members are beginning to only be referred to in association with your show business child, make special efforts to show them that they are important in-and-of themselves. They have their own unique identity that must be fostered and maintained and their association with their famous family member is no more than a frame of reference and does not embody who they are. Protecting your family's personal image and privacy will make their adjustment to your show business child's career pursuits go more smoothly and keep your family safe, whole, and happy.

In this digital age of social networking and the Internet, how can I best protect my child's safety and privacy?

With the institution of social networking sites, any person can put his or her thoughts and actions out there on the Internet for the whole world to read. Facebook, Twitter, Tumblr, and even YouTube provide the public with an endless feed of information regarding the most intimate details of peoples' daily lives. This ability to disseminate thoughts and information with ease may be both a blessing and a curse for your child's career. As your child begins to gain some notoriety, he or she may want to create Facebook and Twitter accounts to garner support from those outside his or her immediate social circles. The more "friends" and "followers" your child has, the bigger his or her fan base. Casting directors, booking agents, and the like will judge your child's popularity on such statistics and possibly allow them to affect their decisions on whether to give your child certain opportunities. In addition, social networking tools will also be a useful means of keeping in touch with your child's fans. Today, fans like to feel close to the performers they admire. Keeping your child's fans "in the loop" about the steps he or she is taking in his or her career, or even simply giving them a glimpse into your child's thoughts (e.g., favorite color, thoughts on a book he or she read) will promote fan loyalty and support.

Teach Responsibility

Such tools, however, are just that: tools. They must be used properly and prudently to best promote your child's career. A single mistake or incident of "loose fingers" will potentially result in millions of people knowing private details about your child's life, or lead to a whirlwind of negative press. It is your job, as parent, to monitor and limit the information your child puts forth online. You must explain to your child that anything he or she writes or uploads onto the Internet *will* be seen and read by the world. Therefore, your child must be very careful and selective about what he or she posts. While your child is still young, it is best if you, your spouse, or a trusted "team" member controls the postings on your child's social media accounts. As your child gets older, he or she may want to have access to the account. At this juncture, reemphasize the expansive nature of the online audience and the importance of filtering what he or she posts. Request that your child run any postings by you, and if he or she is unsure about the appropriateness of a specific post, to simply opt not to post it. Explain and give suggestions of appropriate posts. Updates about upcoming performances or excitement about movie debuts, for example, are enough to keep fans in the know about your child's career. Non-intimate facts or generic opinions your child wishes to share ("My mom just made her famous macaroni and cheese . . . Yum! My favorite!") are acceptable as well. Emphasize, however, that your child must make sure that his or her words are not too personal and could not be misconstrued or found offensive. Another important thing to keep in mind when deciding on an acceptable post is whether the post violates any confidentiality clause in a contract your child is bound by. Many agreements stipulate that your child is not to make any statements regarding aspects of a project before a formal release is disseminated. If such a clause is in effect, your child may face consequences if he or she reveals confidential aspects via the Internet.

Safety Concerns

Not only could this lack of privacy affect your child's image, but it could also threaten your child's safety. With private information easily accessible online, anyone who wishes to cause your child harm or harass him or her may do so with a simple Google search for your child's whereabouts or contact information. Monitoring your child's posts to ensure no such personal information is available to the public is one way to prevent anyone from "tracking down" your child, be they dangerous persons or overly enthusiastic fans. Maintaining this protective separation from the public will enhance your child's sense of security and make him or her feel safe and comfortable as he or she continues down the road to a successful show business career.

CHAPTER 8

Potholes and Speed Traps

ANY JOURNEY WORTH UNDERTAKING IS fraught with peril, and your child's journey into the world of entertainment is no different. You will be tasked with guiding your child to the correct people and avoiding personal and professional roadblocks such as scam artists and outsiders who will seek to take advantage of your child's talent. Beyond that, your child will need you to make the right choices for his or her professional, social, and intellectual development. Tremendous pressure will be exerted on your child from all angles: friends, family, people in the industry, and even yourself. You must find a way to keep your child's best interests in mind when you make decisions without succumbing to these pressures.

How can I avoid scams?

The path to your child's success is akin to an ice-covered roadway. To avoid a crash on the road, you move slowly, exercise caution, and always keep your eyes on the road. Avoiding a scam in the entertainment industry is no different; if you simply keep your eyes on the road and remain cautious, you will almost certainly stay on the right path. Exercising caution in this context means thoroughly investigating any school, camp, instructor, class, or tutor that you consider hiring. If you are hiring an acting coach, ask for references. Speak to people who have used that instructor previously and ask them not only if the service was to their satisfaction, but also whether it was worth the expense. You should be wary of so-called professionals that ask for significant sums of money up front, as these carry the highest risk for being scams. If your child has an agent or manager you have been working with, ask them for recommendations for a singing or acting coach. Seek out registered agents and professionals recommended in trusted industry publications or on the equivalent websites. The guiding principle here is to adequately research your decisions; the more knowledge you obtain about the instructors you are choosing from, the less likely you are to become the victim of a scam.

What are ways I can protect my child from the pressures and "bad habits" of the industry?

Anyone with any knowledge of show business has heard the horror stories of child stars whose lives spiral out of control. Drugs, alcohol, and the party lifestyle are commonplace for many within the industry, and the pressures to partake in them run rampant. Without a good, solid base of morality, values, and self-respect, it is easy for a young, impressionable performer to fall victim to these perils.

One step to take to safeguard your child from falling victim to these dangerous habits is to make sure your child is aware that they exist. Educate your child on the harms of drugs, drinking, gambling, and so forth and that there will be times where he or she will be pressured to partake in one of those activities. Whatever you do, do not simply pretend that pressures like drugs and alcohol do not exist. Teach your child that it is ok to "say no," and keep an open dialogue with him or her with regard to such vices.

Encourage your child to find positive role models within the industry to look to as examples of who he or she should aspire to become. With positive influences, your child will be more inclined to avoid dangerous activities and reason that "because 'so-and-so' wouldn't do it, neither should I."

As always, remain aware of your child's activities. Keep an eye on the people he or she surrounds him- or herself with to ensure your child is surrounded by positive influences. The entertainment industry has a reputation for breeding unsavory characters, and it is easy for your child to be seduced by their charm and submit to peer pressure.

Know where and with whom your child is at all times, and enforce the traditional rules, such as a curfew, that you would enforce on your child if he or she were not pursuing a career in entertainment. Just because your child is "becoming a star" does not mean he or she is above the rules and discipline that build the foundation of a grounded, well-behaved individual.

Know When to Seek Help

In the unfortunate case you discover your child is developing a problem or has partaken in the "drugs, sex, and rock and roll" culture of the entertainment industry, it is time for you to step up and engage the strong hand of parental discipline. Although you may be tempted to be in denial of your child's missteps, overlooking his or her actions and habits will only cause him or her more harm. There is no shame in seeking help. Your child is only human and subject to the same inclinations and temptations as the rest. In fact, it is a rather courageous act to make a decision to turn one's life around. Confront your child immediately about his or her actions, and immediately work to get him or her back on the road to a healthy life. Be careful, however, not to sound harsh and accusatory, as this may have the adverse effect of pushing your child further into this unhealthy lifestyle. Be gentle but firm in your approach and help your child understand how he or she must make changes to eliminate these vices from his or her life, or face serious, often fatal consequences.

Emancipation

There may come a point where, despite your best efforts at being a prudent parent, your child may succumb to the influences of others and be made to believe that *you* are the source of his or her problems. In cases such as this, your child may seek emancipation. In becoming an emancipated minor, a child is legally freed from control by his or her parents. (The parents are freed from any responsibilities for the child as well.) The guidelines and requirements for emancipation vary by state, but generally, parental consent is required except in cases of parental misconduct. If your child decides to file for emancipation without your consent, he or she must petition the juvenile court and provide proof of certain requirements. Again, these requirements vary by state, but, for sake of example, the state of New York requires that the child must meet the following:

- Be over the age of 16

- Not live with either parent (unless they live away from home only because of school, camp, college, or other temporary situation)

- Not receive any financial support from their parents (unless a court has ordered them to pay support or the child only receive benefits that they are entitled to, such as Social Security)

- Have his or her own permanent job as a main source of income

- Not be in foster care or under court-ordered supervision (i.e., not a ward of the state)

The judge will then determine if emancipation is appropriate. It is usually quite difficult to secure emancipation without parental consent, but in the case that the situation has spiraled out of control so much that your child does seek it, it is worthwhile for you, as a prudent parent, to be aware of it.[19]

With positive role models, increased awareness, and a little guidance from you, your child will avoid joining the ranks of tabloid celebrities whose lives have spiraled out of control and will maintain a happy, healthy life and career.

How do I keep my child "grounded" in an industry of big egos, big spending, and big expectations?

As previously discussed, keeping your child grounded will not be an easy task, as children in the entertainment industry do not lead normal lives. This discrepancy with the way most other children come of age can produce feelings of superiority and ultimately leave the child worse-off. The way to combat the possibility of your child's ego inflating beyond the point of no return is through balance. Your child's career is important, and it will require a lot of time and energy to bring it to a successful conclusion, but it is vital that you create a foundation that firmly roots the child to the normal life experiences of a non-entertainer.

Keep a Social Life Alive

A child needs to develop friends and a life outside of the industry in order to remain a well-balanced individual. The first way to accomplish this goal is to keep your child in school for as long as possible. For young children, school is the keystone to building friendships and interacting with others in a normal social environment. Constructing relationships outside of the entertainment industry will provide perspective on what life is like for a child who does not work in the entertainment industry and should be encouraged. Family is the second important piece to keeping your child grounded while working in the industry. As mentioned earlier, you must insist upon the usual course of family life without giving your child special treatment. The entertainment industry is an ego-driven business; do not allow family to foster or fuel that within your child. Enforce normal family rules or obligations such as chores or an allowance. This will not only provide a spending limit and demonstrate the value of money to your child, something sorely lacking in the lives of many young entertainers, but provide a common base of experiences that the child will share with others his or her age.

Maintain Normalcy

Another good way to ensure your child makes friends and is immersed into a normal social setting is through the development of a hobby. Again the key concept is balance: show business should not be the only thing your child does outside of school, even if he or she loves it. Whether it is sports or a school club, ensuring that your child has interests outside of the entertainment industry will help to keep him or her from becoming too swept up in work. Children need to know that there are options outside of show business for them and that if they are unhappy, they have other skills and interests to lean on as well.

Find a Role Model

Finally, look to role models to mentor your children and provide a positive example for them to follow. Too often, we read only about the "bad" examples set by young stars. Though your child will undoubtedly be aware of these individuals who have chosen a "darker path," do not allow them to be the models for your child's behavior. Instead, encourage your child to learn from the mistakes of others, and explain to them the repercussions of making poor decisions and giving in to the hubris of stardom. Seek out families with young stars who have not succumbed to the temptations that fame and glory can present. Making use of the ideas and methods they have employed will help you and your child to steer clear of the many "speed traps" of the industry.

How can I help my child deal with rejection?

Helping your child deal with rejection brings the earlier concept of preparation back to the forefront. "An ounce of prevention is worth a pound of cure" is the guiding principle here. The entertainment industry is the most competitive culture imaginable; if your child cannot learn to handle rejection early in his or her career, then it is time to get out. In entertainment, rejection is simply par for the course—it happens to everyone almost every day. While you do not want to remove all hope, temper your child's expectations so that he or she does not have an unrealistic view of the chances of landing a part. The odds of getting the role being auditioned for, regardless of how talented your child may be, are always going to be small. Furthermore, as Ron Schaefer emphasizes, sometimes failing to land a role may have more to do with what's in the casting director's mind versus the child's talent. However, if you have forewarned your child, the unavoidable rejection will be far easier to bear when it does occur.

While warning your child of the odds, also focus on the process and not the result. Human beings often learn more from failure than from achievement. Explain to your child that rejection is only a necessary pit stop on the road to success, and guide the child's focus to loving the craft itself. Just as a child can enjoy playing baseball or football and never make the all-star team, encourage your child to enjoy the auditions, meetings, and performances even if they do not get the part. Ideally the hard work you and your child put in should be enjoyable learning experiences, not just an awful grind to trudge through before each audition. Landing the part is secondary; orient your child to always take something away from every experience and focus primarily on learning and improvement. This will help to keep your child focused and happy in situations where it can be very easy to become discouraged and disenchanted.

As a proud parent, there may be times you will want to blame others for your child's rejections. It is important to avoid voicing such accusations to or in the presence of your child, as it may condition him or her to see others as the problem and prevent your child from seeking to improve his or her own talents in hopes of "doing better next time." Ron Schaefer of French Woods Camp often finds that parents who tell their children that it is the camp's fault that they were not cast as leads can be incredibly destructive to their child's future. He recalls parents who have even gone so far as to remove their child from French Woods to enroll him or her at another camp that promised the child a lead in every camp production. Ron points out that rejection is an important part of the business from which children interested in a career in music and entertainment should not be sheltered. By making excuses for your child, you deprive them of a crucial learning and growth experience.

As always, however, if you do discover that your child does not handle rejection well and cannot simply "enjoy the ride," walk away. It is not worth jeopardizing your and your child's happiness for a tiny chance at success.

What do I do if a job requires my child to do something I feel is inappropriate?

The simple answer is to not allow the child do whatever is being asked of him or her. Say something to the director or casting director about being uncomfortable with what is happening. They may be able to put your worries to rest, but if they cannot, then do not put your child in a situation that you will both regret down the line. You have an obligation to make responsible decisions for your child, and if you are not 100 percent comfortable with what is being asked of him or her, then the job is not worth the risk. The physical and mental health and safety of your child are second to no other consideration, and you have both the right and responsibility to safeguard those interests.

The difficulty in getting out is not the act of removing your child from the industry but coming to grips with the fact that despite the money or fame, what is best for your child is to call it quits. You are the adult; you must make the decision as to when it is time to get out. Realizing when that time has come is easier if you have a strong management team in place with whom you have an open, candid relationship. If you suspect that your child is unhappy, speak to your child's agent, manager, and lawyer about it. Communication is vital to making such an important determination. The more honest you are with your team, your child, and yourself, the easier it will be to decide when it is time to walk away. This may well be a very difficult decision, but remember that when your child is not enjoying what he or she is doing is most often when things begin to spiral downward personally and professionally. The peril is simply too great for you to allow your child to continue working if in reality he or she wants to stop.

CHAPTER 9

Alternate Routes

How can advances in technology help me raise money and cut the costs associated with launching my child's career?

YOU ARE IN LUCK! As previously discussed, there are alternatives to involving intimidating gatekeepers such as record companies and distributors in order to get your child's career underway. Today's entertainment industry is experiencing a New Renaissance Paradigm of do-it-yourself (DIY) creative and distribution techniques. Artists are no longer exclusively subject to the heavy-handed rule (and expenses) of the major distributors, producers, and record labels in order to maintain a sustainable career. New business models and marketing techniques are available to help these artists keep their hands on the wheel and control their own success. In this New Renaissance Paradigm, the creator can take a detour around the institutional middleman—once the gatekeeper controlling access to audiences, media, and creative facilities—and take a direct route to these targets. New advances in technology enable content creators to utilize new modes of marketing and distributing their product by using social media outlets, such as YouTube and Facebook, to disseminate the material to a wider audience than would traditionally be reached via an institutional label or distributor. Artists such as Justin Bieber, Greyson Chance, and Rebecca Black have become singing sensations by taking advantage of digital platforms like YouTube to get their materials out to the world and showcase their talents. Your child, too, can take advantage of the new paradigms in entertainment.

Record Label

As an alternative to chasing down existing major record labels, you can consider using websites like Dittomusic to set up your own record label. Services offered include distribution streams, as well as 100 percent right to royalties. This alternative to the traditional music industry route can result in tremendous cost-savings, such as getting a single on iTunes for free, and, for a very low fee, having a song distributed through two hundred streaming and download sources worldwide, including Spotify, Amazon, and Zune. Albums compare at $30, while ringtone distribution is free. Freedom is also valued by Ditto in the sense that joining the site is completely non-exclusive, and the site permits an opt out at any time, should a record deal become more attractive and available to your child.[20] Artists such as Sam Smith, Ed Sheeran, and Sarah McLachlan have utilized this platform and met with great success.[21]

Crowdfunding

Despite the tremendous savings creating your own record label may generate, your personal funds may still be inadequate to cover other costs, such as recording your child's music should you choose to distribute it on a site like Dittomusic. That's where crowdfunding sites like Kickstarter, Indiegogo, and ChipIn come in. Some of these fundraising sites give the option to send funds directly to your PayPal account, making fundraising even easier. These alternative routes to a successful career in music and entertainment are at your fingertips when you open up your web browser. Using sites like YouTube, Facebook, and Twitter to promote your child's talent will help maximize potential contributors to your fundraising efforts. Musician Julia Nunes has come a long way from beginning piano lessons at age seven to progressing to writing her own music on guitar at age fourteen to becoming an Internet sensation based on YouTube videos featuring her performing songs with her signature ukulele. For that reason, CNN has profiled Julia's success in posting homemade music videos to her YouTube page, which resulted in approximately 40 million views.[22] Julia used the momentum she built on YouTube to amass 61,269 fans on Facebook.[23] In June 2011, Julia launched a Kickstarter campaign to raise $15,000 to defray some of the costs associated with recording an album; however, Julia astonishingly raised $78,888, which she was able to apply toward her latest album, *Settle Down*.[24] Now that you are educated on the resources available on the Internet, you can also choose to point and click your child's way to success.

Home Studio

Another way to lower the costs associated with recording an album is by creating a home studio. Producer Jimmy Landry advocates investing as little as $300 to buy software and equipment to create a home studio for your musically-inclined child rather than spending $50 per hour and signing contracts with a producer you do not know. The elements of a home studio include the following: (1) a great microphone; (2) a great preamp to plug your microphone into; (3) an interface (e.g., a Roland Octo-capture), which translates audio to visual; (4) a digital audio workstation for your family's Mac (Garage Band already included) or PC (Sonar software can be purchased for approximately $100); and (5) monitors, which can be SD6 speakers or even a pair of headphones. Although there is a learning curve associated with your child learning how to record his or her own music at home, it may be equated to children mastering the latest video game. You may hire professionals to set up your home studio who will teach you and your child how to use it. Additionally, if you purchase your home studio from Sweetwater, they have telephone service that will assist you with all aspects of using the equipment. Local music stores are incentivized to help you with your operational questions because as you become successful and want to upgrade your equipment, you are likely to be their best customers. Finally, there are many resources available online, and videos posted to YouTube can provide tutorials on frequently asked questions like how to get the right level for your microphone. Investing in a simple home studio upfront may provide exponential savings over the course of your child's career as a musician. Additionally, it teaches children more about the technical aspect of their desired career.

Online Media Platforms

Using online resources and crowdfunding platforms is not limited to the pursuit of a career in music. They also prove useful in other areas of entertainment, such as acting and filmmaking. Platforms such as the above mentioned Indiegogo and Seed&Spark[25] target the film industry specifically. Not unlike raising money for recording an album, your child can create a page for his or her film to raise the funds necessary for the equipment and other expenses necessary to produce it. It is important to note, however, that like any other crowdfunding project, your child must put in much effort to market his or her page and raise awareness around the campaign. This can be done through promoting the crowdfunding site on his or her own social media accounts, sharing a link through postings on other accounts, and simply asking friends and family to promote the project through their own social media channels.

If your child is pursuing a career in acting, online channels such as YouTube and Vimeo can be key in getting him or her recognized and establishing an initial fan base. Your creative child can develop one-off videos or even his or her own webseries on these Internet-based platforms, establishing him- or herself as an online personality and gaining attention in that sphere. Garnering enough attention here can lead to opportunities in the mainstream film and television industry. For example, actress Jessica Rose began her career as LonelyGirl15 on YouTube. She developed a following as a teen girl who posted videos about her personal thoughts on life, becoming an online "personality." What seemed like an unscripted video diary turned out to actually be a fictional web series produced by Jessica and film-savvy friends. With the help of her YouTube success, Jessica went on to play a role in the ABC Family television series *Greek* and has appeared in several movies.[26]

These online platforms can also prove useful in helping your child get his or her foot in the door in the film and television industry (or even in live theater) by giving your child the ability to audition for a role that time constraints or location might otherwise preclude him or her from pursuing. Many casting agents allow for video submissions of auditions, eliminating the roadblock to auditions in, for example, Los Angeles, that would otherwise be inaccessible to a child actor in Wisconsin. In addition, websites such as WIX.com and SquareSpace allow your child to easily create his or her own website where your child can feature his or her résumé, photos, articles, reel strip, and any other videos or media he or she would like casting agents to see.

The breakdown of the "location barrier" to entry by way of online platforms holds true throughout the entertainment industry, regardless of whether your child is pursuing a career in music, acting, or another entertainment form. It is no longer imperative that your child be based in one of the major entertainment hubs such as New York and Los Angeles. The power of using Internet platforms for getting a start can even cross oceans. For example, singer/songwriter Peppina[27] made use of the collaborative online production company HitRECord[28] to amass a following and distribute her music to people all over the world. Through this website, Peppina, hailing from Helsinki, Finland, has been able to establish a fan base across the Atlantic and is now gaining renown in the United States.

Although it is likely that as your child's career takes off, he or she will have to be more conveniently located, Peppina's online success story, along with those of many others, demonstrate that your child can start his or her journey from right where he or she is.

I have much experience in other areas of business. Can I use my knowledge and skills to help further my child's career in this manner?

Of course you can! However, the same caution must be taken as if you were to take on the role of your child's manager. You must keep your role as "professional parent" separate from your role navigating your child's career. In this New Renaissance Paradigm, it is even more important for you, the parent, to have a clear view of the road ahead because you are steering the car with no seasoned industry institutions serving as backseat drivers. As long as you maintain good business practices, you and your child will still be on the right road, albeit an alternate one, to a successful career in music and entertainment.

As any good businessperson knows, it is crucial for a business to stay current and informed about advances within its relevant fields. With you and your child now in control of his or her career, it is up to you to become knowledgeable about the new business models and marketing strategies enabled by this New Renaissance Paradigm. A wonderful thing about new Internet technologies is that you can read about them . . . on the Internet. There are many online entertainment industry periodicals and blogs that discuss cutting-edge technologies and business models for independent artists and performers. A simple search will reveal sources such as *IndieGuide, TGDaily, Wired,* and *VentureBeat,* which give real-time updates on new advances in entertainment technology and business. Keep an open mind when reading about strategies used by other performers in your child's field of entertainment. What may work for one person may not work for your child's goals or abilities; thus, you must tailor the strategies of others to create a customized business model for your child's career. Remember, however, that you will create the best business model when fully informed of all avenues available to you and your child. Stay current and well read on innovations within the industry, and you can be the skillful driver of your child's show business career.

Every good business maintains a steady stream of production and innovation. Your child's career should be no different. When self-distributing and promoting your child in his or her career, it is important to ensure that your child keeps creating and developing new content to disseminate to the masses via the available channels. Because videos, music, photos, and so forth can be posted and viewed online in an instant, an audience can quickly "get bored" of old content, even if it is only a few weeks or days old, and want more to get their fix. If your child fails to provide his or her fan base with a constant stream of updates, he or she may lose fan loyalty, and the DIY distribution strategy could fail. This does not mean your child must be writing and recording songs or videos to post on his or her YouTube channel every day. A simple "tweet" on Twitter or blog post on his or her website may suffice as long as it signals that your child is still "there" and wants to keep connected to his or her fans. Additionally, renowned acting instructor Ken Feinberg suggests that parents consider executive producing or self-producing a short film or web series starring your child to increase his or her exposure.

This being said, make sure the content your child does put out via these alternate channels is of the caliber and quality of content that would be disseminated by the traditional corporate producers, distributors, and labels, which means keeping up-to-date with your child's peers who are represented by major record labels. A business is only as good as its product, and unprofessional content will damage your child's career prospects. Always review and edit the materials your child records or writes before sending it out to the viral universe of the Internet where it can be met with harsh and hurtful criticism and negative publicity. If you are unsure or simply wish to be cautious in your choices, consult a trusted friend or any other person with experience in your child's particular field of the entertainment industry, such as a member of your "team" (i.e., an attorney or talent coach). Be sure, however, that you can trust whoever you ask to provide his or her unbiased and honest opinion, not simply to placate you and your child with niceties. A second set of eyes and ears can prevent damage from an embarrassing posting that cannot easily be reversed. By only distributing your child's best content, you ensure that he or she creates an image defined by creativity, talent, and professionalism. These three qualities provide a basis for a successful business: your child's show business career.

Bookkeeping

Every good business has a prudent bookkeeper; thus, it is important to stay organized and diligent, closely monitoring all outlets through which you distribute your child's material to the public. Although keeping your hands on the wheel rather than handing control of your child's career over to the major distributors, producers, and labels will eliminate the risk of not being given enough attention by the relevant institution, it leaves the door open to possible neglect or distraction on your part. Since managing the content distribution and audience access aspects of your child's career is most likely not your full-time job, it can be easy to become sidetracked and, for lack of a better term, "slack off" on the maintenance and monitoring of these outlets. To prevent this pitfall, schedule time each week to review traffic and "hits" on your child's online media outlets. Keeping track of your crowdfunding sites is extremely crucial. Not only do these sites help increase your child's popularity and fan base, but they can also provide the bread-and-butter funds that will enable your child to keep pursuing his or her career without the aid of industry gatekeeper corporations. Note the data in a log so that you and your child can track the progress of his or her career and monitor where additional efforts must be made to increase popularity. This practice has an added benefit of getting your child involved in the management of his or her own career so that, when the time comes for your child to take the wheel, he or she will already know how to drive his or her career down the path to success via this alternate route in the New Renaissance Paradigm of the entertainment industry.

CHAPTER 10

Arrival: Reaching the Destination

My child has established a successful entertainment career—what now?

Congratulations! You have accomplished a feat that all parents hope to see their children achieve. You have helped your child realize his or her dream. Now is your chance to sit back and relish your child's happiness. Take the time to truly watch your child in his or her element as he or she does what they do best: perform!

Although your hard work is finally paying off, this is not the time to allow your child's career to simply coast down the road on cruise control. Now your child's "goal" has become a career, and it must still be treated as a business just like any other job. It is important to continue to keep track of finances, maintain business relationships, and employ team members in whom you trust and feel will keep your child's career on the road to success. As previously mentioned, it may become helpful to add new team members, such as publicists and stylists, to maintain your child's image. As your child's journey progresses, you will encounter more in-depth legal issues, so be sure to keep a trusted attorney on hand to offer his or her legal guidance with these more difficult matters. Continue to keep up on all of the practices you followed to get to this point in your child's career. Just because the car has survived the journey does not mean you do not have to continue its maintenance and upkeep.

Just as you must continue to manage the business side of your child's career, so must you monitor your child's happiness and well-being. Keep an eye on your child's enthusiasm, and maintain an open dialogue with him or her about his or her feelings toward his or her career. Ask your child's opinion on what direction he or she would like to see his or her career go in, and help to guide it in that direction, provided that you, too, believe it is a good choice for your child. There will be times when your child may not express to you his or her discontent or even recognize that his or her career is compromising his or her physical or mental health. You, as a parent, must always remain vigilant and keep an eye out for warning signs that signal trouble for your child, such as exhaustion, stress, or negative influences. As stressed throughout this book, you are first and foremost a parent, and your little "star" is first and foremost your child. As New York agent Nancy Carson expresses in her book *Raising A Star*, "[A] good professional parent is one who helps her child further his career goals without sacrificing the child's personal growth."[29] His or her happiness and health are your main priorities, and you must provide for these no matter how successful your child becomes.

Higher education

A significant matter not yet mentioned is that of your child's higher education. As your child progresses in his or her entertainment career, he or she may become so consumed by the prospect of stardom that college becomes the farthest thing from your child's mind. The spotlight of show business can outshine any spark of interest in achieving a degree from a respected university. A lifetime of success in entertainment is not always a guarantee, and your child may someday have to face the unfortunate reality that his or her career in the spotlight is over. When the music ends and the lights go out, your child may be left floundering for a new direction in life. By stressing the importance of achieving a college degree, this uncertainty and lack of direction can be avoided, and your child will be left well equipped to take an alternative route to making a happy and lucrative living. A degree will provide your child with additional skills and knowledge necessary to pursue a career outside of performing. It will allow your child to explore the world outside the entertainment industry or even let him or her navigate the entertainment world with more insight and business savvy. Keep your child's higher education in the forefront of his or her mind. Continue to emphasize the importance of education, and encourage your child to work hard in school and get good grades so that he or she may have many options once it comes time for him or her to apply to schools. A busy touring and traveling schedule may be a blessing in disguise, as it enables you and your child to visit colleges across the country along the way.

College does not have to be an option exclusive to your child's pursuit of his or her performance career. Getting a degree in a related field from a reputable institution may give your child that added edge and skill that will help to advance his or her performance career. Casting director Adrienne Stern notes that a college degree may enhance your child's talents by providing him or her with unique life experiences to base his or her performances on or refer to for motivation. She frequently sees former child actors who do not go to college be eclipsed by their peers with college degrees when they audition for the same role because they lack the life experience college provides.

Should your child be interested in pursuing an undergraduate degree in a performance field, such as theater, you may want to consider using an acting or other performance coach to help best prepare your child so that he or she may secure admission at a prestigious institution. Acting coach Lisbeth Bartlett, who has a reputation for preparing high school students for the audition component of their college application, notes that her specialized pre-college coaching has helped talented young actors secure admittances at prestigious programs such as New York University's Tisch School of the Arts. Receiving the proper training and preparation will provide your child with the best chance possible of being selected to take part in a reputable program, thus enhancing his or her skills and, in turn, providing your child with an advantage in his or her performance career.

In addition to providing career-enhancing experience, a college degree will also give your child the option of supplementing his or her performance by someday expanding into the business, production, or representation side of the entertainment industry. A major in business, film, music production, or a similar field will allow your child to someday take the reins and be the one "calling the shots" in show business. With the security of having earned a college degree, there is no limit to what your child can achieve.

When do I let my child take control of his or her own career?

There will come a point in time when your child will want to have more control over the management of his or her career. As your child grows older, usually beginning around the rebellious teenage years, your child will feel that it is he or she who knows best about the workings of his or her career and that you are no longer necessary to help guide it along the path to success. Though it is true that your child may grow in general maturity and knowledge as he or she grows older, it is unlikely that your child will have the business mindset and industry savvy needed to navigate the often-tricky road to show business success that has been riddled with such potholes as mentioned earlier. Although your child has been the focus of his or her career thus far, meaning that it was he or she who attended all the auditions, tapings, movie shoots, performances, and so on, this does not mean that your child is thoroughly prepared to take on the management aspect. Young people lack life experience; thus, they may not have yet developed a strong sense of good judgment. They may still be naïve and trusting, making them easy prey for the sharks and vultures that riddle the entertainment world, trying to take advantage of young performers. Therefore, when your child begins to want to take on a greater role in the management of his or her career, do not simply sit back in the passenger seat, close your eyes, and relax while your child drives, trying to navigate on his or her own. When your child begins to push you away, prepare him or her to take the wheel by teaching the fundamentals of managing the career. Impart upon him or her all of the knowledge you yourself have gained by experience while helping your child achieve his or her entertainment career. Share with your child the nuances and idiosyncrasies of the industry that you have learned so that, gradually, your child can take over. By training your child in this manner, as an apprentice, he or she will have a better understanding of what is required of him or her if he or she is to maintain his or her own career.

Even when your child is prepared and of age (a "safe" estimate is eighteen, the age of majority) to take over his or her own career, and you feel comfortable playing a far lesser role, do not leave your child on his or her own. Ensure that your child has a group of advisors whom he or she can trust to help him or her along the way. These advisors may already be a part of your team of professionals, in which case they are likely to be people you trust. If your child brings a new advisor into the mix, do your research, and keep an eye on him or her until you are comfortable that he or she is someone that has your child's best interests at heart. And, of course, ensure your child knows that no matter what happens, he or she can always turn to you for guidance and help. As a parent, you are always there for your child and will continue to provide him or her with support, no matter what his or her age or status.

An important aspect of allowing your child to handle his or her career is his or her ability to legally sign and ratify contracts. As mentioned earlier, in most states, New York included, a contract signed by a minor, under the age of eighteen, is either void or voidable by that minor (unless it is for a "necessity" such as food, shelter, or clothing). Therefore, until your child reaches that age, he or she will need you to sign any agreements. When both of you sign together, your child is bound and liable for any violation of the terms of the contract. He or she can no longer disaffirm the contract if you have given your consent for your child, as long as it is determined that you did so in his or her best interest. In addition to the ability to be bound to a contract, when your child reaches age eighteen, he or she is able to ratify the terms of any contract he or she signed before reaching that age. If, after turning eighteen, your child keeps performing according to the terms of a contract he or she signed while still a minor, he or she will be considered to have ratified the contract and will be bound by it.

It remains your responsibility to thoroughly review every aspect of anything you and your child sign or, better yet, to consult an attorney before signing so that he or she may explain to you and your child exactly what is covered by the contract and ensure that your child is thoroughly protected. Your attorney may also negotiate with the other party so that the agreement includes terms more favorable to your child. Even once your child reaches age eighteen, stress to him or her the importance of not being pressured into signing anything until it has been thoroughly reviewed and understood. Make sure your child maintains a relationship with your attorney in this respect so that you know that someone is in place to protect your child even though you are no longer in control of his or her career.

Just because your child has taken over control of his or her career doesn't mean you wash your hands of all involvement. It is important for you to still show interest in his or her progress and provide your child with as much support and encouragement as you always have. Furthermore, you are not relieved of your duty as parent to ensure that your child stays safe, happy, and healthy throughout his or her life. Keep a vigilant watch over your child's well-being, and remember always to be there when your child needs a hand. Although your child now has his or her license to drive, you do not have to take both of your hands off the wheel. You can now sit back and enjoy the ride . . . but don't fall asleep!

Operating Manual

IF YOU HAVE ANY QUESTIONS while navigating the road toward your child's success in music and entertainment, you may want to consult this operating manual, which compiles online resources as well key terms you can expect to see in music and entertainment contracts.

I. **RESOURCES**

- Steven C. Beer, Entertainment Attorney - http://www. stevenbeer.com/

- BizParentz Foundation - Supporting Families of Children Working In The Entertainment Industry: http://www.bizparentz.org/ home.html

- Entertainment Jobs, Auditions, Casting Notices, Résumés and Demo Reels - Backstage.com: http://casting.backstage.com/ jobseekerx/

- Adrienne Stern Casting: http://www.adriennestern.com/

- Barry Klarberg, CPA - Monarch Wealth & Business Management: http://www.monarchmgmtllc.com/

- Beth Melsky Casting: http://www.bethmelsky.com/about.html

- Brian Thomas, Choreographer: http://www.brianthomasinc.com/

- Cakewalk - The World's Best Software for Recording and Making Music on PC and Mac: http://www.cakewalk.com/

- Cari Cole - Helping New Music Artists Find Their Voice, Craft Their Style and Create Successful Music Careers: http://www. caricole.com/

- Creative Studios of Atlanta: http://www.creativestudiosofatlanta.com/

- Eileen DeNobile - Nobile Talent Management: http://nobletalentmanagement.com/experience

- Emily Grace Productions - Think Like a Producer, Act For a Living: http://emilygrace.tv/

- Errol Wander, CPA - Specializing in Entertainment Business Management and Tour Accounting: http://www.pragerfenton.com/about/leadership/errol-wander.php

- French Woods Festival - A Performing Arts Summer Camp: http://www.frenchwoods.com/

- Harvey Tanton, CPA - Specializing in the Recording, Motion Picture and Video Production Industries: http://tantoncpas.com/page.jsp?content=Home&decider=dhoffman2

- Iliana Kadushin - Actor, Singer, Producer, Voice-Over Artist: http://www.ilyanakadushin.com/

- John Germain Leto - The Rockstar in You Blog: http://rockstarinyou.wordpress.com/about/

- Lara Jill Miller – Voice-Over Actress Famous for Work on Children's Cartoons: http://www.larajillmiller.net/voiceover.html

- Larry Rudolph Management - ReignDeer Entertainment: http://www.reign-deer.com/

- Lisbeth Bartlett, Private Acting Coach - Expert Coaching for School and Professional Auditions: http://www.lisbethbartlett.com/

II. **ESSENTIAL TERMS OF A MANAGEMENT AGREEMENT**

TERM.

- Initial term generally 3 years.

- May provide for automatic renewals unless either party gives written notice of its election to terminate within 30 days.

- May be tied to album releases or tour schedules.

SERVICES.

- Selection of literary, artistic, and musical material.

- Publicity, public relations and advertising.

- General practices in the entertainment industry regarding such matters as manager has knowledge, such as compensation and privileges extended for similar artistic services.

- Selection of, and negotiation with, agencies and other third parties that seek and procure employment and engagements for artists.

- Selection of, and negotiation with, any and all potential users of your talents.

- You and Manager shall promptly inform each other of all offers of employment, and of all inquiries concerning your career, so that manager may determine and advise you whether same are compatible with your career.

- Manager is not licensed as an agent.

- No promise or obligation to procure any employment or engagements.

- You shall be solely responsible for payment of all necessary commissions to booking or similar agencies.

MANAGER'S AUTHORITY.

- Approve and permit any and all publicity and advertising.

- Approve the use of your name, photograph, likeness, voice, sound effects, caricatures, literary, artistic and musical materials solely for purposes of advertising and publicity and in the promotion and advertising of your products and services.

  - In that regard, you shall have the right to approve any likeness and biographical materials before manager approves its use (provided that such approval shall not be unreasonably withheld).

- Execute for you in your name and/or in your behalf, any and all agreements, documents and contracts for personal appearances, provided that such agreements shall not be for an engagement of more than 3 performances within a 1 week period in connection with a tour.

- Engage as well as discharge in your name, theatrical agents, and employment agencies as well as other persons, firms and corporations who may be retained to obtain contracts and/or engagements for employment for you.

MANAGER'S COMMISSION.

- Generally 10-20 percent of gross income pursuant to agreements entered or negotiated during the term.

- Paid to Manager when said gross income is received by you.

- Any monies due to manager resulting from above, shall be computed after first deducting counsel fees and disbursements.

- Gross income shall be sent to your business manager who shall in turn pay the fee and all expenses along with a statement within 30 days of receiving any gross income.

- Gross income is defined as all forms of income, payments, cash and non-cash consideration, compensation, sums, emoluments or any other thing of value, including, salaries, advances, fees, royalties, bonuses, gifts, shares of receipt, stock and stock options paid to, credited to, or actually received by you (or any corporation, partnership, or other entity in which you have an interest, regardless of by whom procured) as a result of your activities in and throughout the entertainment industry. With respect to live musical performances, gross income shall mean all monies received by you less all bona fide budgeted expenses incurred (following full prior good faith consultation with manager) in relation to such live performance including, but not limited to booking agents' fees, costs of PA and lighting, reasonable transportation and accommodations, and fees and salaries of the road and stage crew.

- Gross income shall not include such excluded monies are sometimes referred to herein as the excluded portion of gross income:

  ○ Income derived from agreements substantially negotiated and entered into after the expiration or termination of the term. In this connection, but not by way of limitation, all agreements substantially negotiated during the term and consummated within 6 months thereafter shall be deemed entered into during the term;

  ○ All music publishing income earned by you that is retained by or paid to third parties, including, without limitation, songwriter royalties payable to co-writers and publishing company administration fees;

  ○ Payments to you under a recording agreement in the nature of recoupable deficit tour support payments to the extent that such payments are actually used by you for such purpose;

  ○ In connection with live performances where monies payable to you include monies payable to a so-called "opening act" (provided that you are not the opening act), such monies as you pay to such opening act;

  ○ Any monies paid to you for recording and video production costs to the extent that such monies are actually used by you for such purpose; and

  ○ Interest earned on gross income following receipt thereof.

- Expenses

  ○ You agree that you shall pay all your expenses, and manager shall not have any liability whatsoever in such connection.

  ○ Manager shall not be required to travel to meet with you at any particular place; however, when manager travels on your behalf, at your request, it shall be at your sole expense.

- You agree to reimburse manager for all expenses, which manager advances or incurs on your behalf hereunder including, but not limited to, the cost of all long distance telephone calls, transportation undertaken by manager at your request or with your consent and all lodging and living expenses connected therewith.

- Manager shall furnish to you a statement of the expenses incurred not less frequently than once in each calendar quarter during the term.

- Manager shall not incur any individual expense (other than expenses incurred for travel) in excess of $500 without your prior approval, provided that such approval shall not be unreasonably withheld or delayed.

AUDIT RIGHTS.

- You agree that manager and manager's representatives may inspect and audit your books and records to ascertain the amounts due.

- Any audit and/or inspection, if any, shall be conducted upon reasonable notice given to you by manager.

INDEPENDENT CONTRACTOR.

- You hereby acknowledge that manager's position hereunder is that of an independent contractor.

- Manager's services are not exclusive to you and manager shall be permitted to perform the same or similar services for other artists or persons during the term.

- Manager shall be permitted to devote such time and efforts to other business activities as manager may deem necessary or desirable, in manager's sole discretion.

INDEMNIFICATION.

- Mutual indemnification clauses like the following are in your best interest.

◦ Each party will indemnify, defend and hold harmless the other party and its affiliates, their respective officers, directors, employees and agents from and against any and all losses, liabilities, claims, obligations, costs and expenses (including reasonable outside attorneys' fees) which result from or arise in connection with or are related in any way to a third party claim resulting from a breach by the indemnifying party of any of its representations and warranties in the agreement; <u>provided</u> such claim has been reduced to a final judgment or settled with the indemnifying party's written consent, not to be unreasonably withheld or delayed.

<u>BREACH</u>.

- If at any time you fail, for any reason whatsoever, to fulfill or perform any obligation assumed by you hereunder, then, without limiting manager's rights, manager shall have the right, exercisable at any time by written notice to you, to extend the expiration date of the then current period of the term.

- Such extension shall continue until you have fully cured such failure or engagement and the then current period of the term shall be extended for a period of time equal to the duration of any such failure.

- You acknowledge that manager's exercise of its rights hereunder shall not in any way affect or diminish its right to equitable relief.

III. **CORE BUILDING BLOCKS OF BECOMING A SUCCESSFUL YOUTUBE CREATOR**

Adapted from YouTube Creator Academy:
https://www.youtube.com/yt/creators/education.html

<u>Core Building Blocks</u>

1. Set goals for your channel.

   a. Have some great ideas for an awesome video or two? It's your turn to share your creativity and start a YouTube channel to call your own. Create some plans for a successful channel and bring your idea to life, with a great set of videos that can thrive on YouTube.

2. Present each of your videos.

   a. First impressions count, and on YouTube, they start with a single video. The first few days after you post a video are critical to its popularity, so make sure you present your video with maximum curb appeal.

3. Get subscribers and entice them to come back to watch more.

   a. Subscribers are your biggest fans and are critical to your success on YouTube! You will want your viewers to subscribe to your channel so they'll come back and watch more.

4. Discovery – Learn how your videos can reach new viewers.

   a. You can make your channel and content more discoverable on YouTube so that your audience can find your videos. Engaging content that your audience enjoys drives watch time and will help your videos show up in search results more often.

5. Understand how YouTube Analytics can help to guide channel decisions.

   a. Learn the basics of YouTube Analytics to get insight into who your viewers are, what they like to watch, and how they engage so you can make informed decisions on how to improve your videos and boost watch time.

IV. SAG/AFTRA SAFETY TIPS FOR YOUNG PERFORMERS

(As seen at http://www.sagaftra.org/content/safety-tips)

SAFETY TIPS

STUNTS AND HAZARDOUS CONDITIONS

1. If a minor is asked to perform any activity that seems hazardous or questionable, the minor is entitled to have the activity performed by a qualified stunt person.

2. It should never be the sole decision of the producer, director, stunt supervisor or any crew member that any activity is safe enough for the child to perform.

3. It is the minor's parent's primary and most important responsibility to ensure the safety of their child.

4. The minor or the minor's parents always has the right to refuse to perform any activity that might be hazardous to the minor, either physically or emotionally.

5. If the minor believes the situation is dangerous or is fearful (whether real or imagined) the minor cannot be required to perform.

6. Parents should request a stunt and safety expert, if the minor is to perform the activity, or a stunt double if necessary.

7. Minors should be acquainted with all first aid personnel (required on all SAG-AFTRA productions) and procedures immediately on arrival.

8. Outdoor shoots often require long periods of time in the elements. Parents should guard minors against dehydration, hypothermia and overexposure to the sun. Parents should not hesitate to contact first aid personnel immediately if the minor is too wet, too cold or too tired.

9. No minor should work in any of these situations without careful supervision by trained technicians and medical personnel.

10. Parents should consider the impact of mature or emotionally difficult dialogue or actions on their child's well-being. Only the parent knows what their child can tolerate and therefore MUST ensure their well-being.

Safety Bulletins

The Industry Wide Labor-Management Safety Committee periodically issues Safety Bulletins that deal with various safety issues. Parents may view these bulletins at http://csatf.org/

PROTECTING YOUR PRIVACY

1. Limit the personal information on a child's résumé and headshot.

2. Use the minor's agent or manager's address or phone number instead of personal information.

3. Do not include the child's school name or other information that can be used to easily locate the child (i.e. shirts with school insignia)

4. Never put Social Security Number on sign in sheets, instead, use your SAG-AFTRA ID number.

V. CBA SAG/ AFTRA – SECTION 50: EMPLOYMENT OF MINORS

http://www.sagaftra.org/files/sag/documents/
cba_employment-of-minors.pdf

50. EMPLOYMENT OF MINORS

A. Preamble

(1) The Producers and Union, recognizing the special situation that arises when minor children are employed, have

formulated the following provisions in addition to those contained in other Sections of this Agreement to ensure that:

(a) The environment in which the performance is to be produced is proper for the minor;

(b) The conditions of employment are not detrimental to the health, morals and safety of the minor; and

(c) The minor's education will not be neglected or hampered by his or her participation in such performance.

(2) Engagement Upon employment of any minor, Producer shall notify the minor's parent or guardian of the terms and conditions of employment, including the name of the Producer, place and duration of location work, if any, and special abilities required. Upon the employment of any minor in any areas outside of California, Producer shall notify the Union of such employment and the area where such employment will take place.

B. It is recognized that when minors are employed in the State of California or taken from the State of California pursuant to a-109 - contractual arrangement made in the State of California, the applicable California laws and regulations shall regulate such employment. When minors are hired and employed within states other than California, the Producer shall be required to determine and comply with the prevailing law governing and defining minors. In addition to these legal requirements for minors not employed in the State of California or not taken from the State of California pursuant to a contractual arrangement made in the State of California, the Producer and the Union agree to the following provisions of Section 50 herein for the employment of minors:

C. Definition of Minor

The term "minor," as used herein, means any performer under the age of eighteen (18) years, except that it shall not include any such performer if: (1) the performer has satisfied the compulsory education laws of the state governing the performer's employment; (2) the performer is married; (3) the performer is a member of the armed forces; or (4) the performer is legally emancipated, in which case it is agreed that both the Producer and the minor shall comply fully with the legal terms of the minor's emancipation.

D. Education

(1) (a) If a minor is guaranteed three (3) or more consecutive days of employment, Producer agrees to employ a teacher, from the first day of such employment, whenever the minor is engaged on any day during which the primary or secondary school regularly attended by the minor is in session. The same shall apply when the Producer's production schedule for a given production plans for scenes to be photographed with the minor on three (3) or more consecutive days. When the minor is employed in scenes planned on the production schedules for only two (2) consecutive days and it is subsequently determined that additional calls will be necessary, Producer shall use its best efforts to provide a teacher on the third consecutive day of such employment or, at the latest, on the fourth consecutive day of such employment and thereafter.

(b) On any day a minor is employed but is not otherwise entitled to have a teacher, the minor shall nevertheless be taught if the primary or secondary school such minor regularly attends is in session and Producer has employed a teacher to instruct another performer engaged on the same production.

(c) If Producer employs a minor for post-production work, no teacher need be provided if the minor's call for such work is after the minor's regular school has been dismissed for the day.

(d) Producer shall provide schooling as required by this Agreement during Producer's workweek for the production.

(2) Such teacher shall have proper teaching credentials appropriate to the level of education required (i.e., primary or secondary level) from Washington D.C. or any state within the United States, but need not be credentialed by or a resident of the state wherein the minor's employment occurs unless otherwise required by law.

(3) The teacher's remuneration shall be paid by Producer.

(4) Producer shall provide a ratio of not more than ten (10) minors per teacher, except that up to twenty (20) minors may be taught per teacher if the minors are in not more than two (2) grade levels.

(5) A teacher may not serve more than one (1) production in any one (1) day, except in an emergency and except as provided in subsection D.(1)(c) above.

(6) If the minor's regular instruction is primarily in a language other than English, teaching in that language will be provided whenever feasible.

(7) However, on any day that the minor is not required to report to the set, the minor may attend his or her regular school, but Producer shall not count more than three (3) hours of the hours attended per day at the minor's regular school as school time for purposes of this Agreement. If the minor's parent or guardian does not choose to have the minor attend regular school on such day, Producer may elect to either teach the minor on the set or in the minor's home or in the home of the teacher employed by Producer, but only if there are no other minors present in the home who are not also being taught by the teacher.

(8) Producer agrees to provide a school facility, such as a schoolhouse, classroom, trailer schoolhouse or other schooling area, which closely approximates the basic requirements for classrooms, especially with respect to adequate lighting, heating, desks and chairs. Stationary buses or cars are

not adequate school facilities unless used exclusively for the minors during instruction. A moving car or bus shall never be used as a school facility; minors must not be taught while being transported to or from local locations.

(9) Producer shall provide schooling equipment and supplies. However, the minor's parent or guardian must, if permitted by the minor's regular school, secure school assignments and the minor's school books for use at the place of employment.

(10) No one shall be allowed in an area being utilized by Producer as a school facility except the teacher and those minors being taught.

(11) The teacher shall determine the required number of hours to be devoted to instruction during a day, but the minor must be taught an average of at least three (3) hours per day, no period of less than twenty (20) minutes duration being acceptable as school time. The maximum number of hours that may be set aside for the minor's instruction in any one (1) day shall be as follows: for kindergarten, four (4) hours; for grades one (1) through six (6), five (5) hours; and for grades seven (7) through twelve (12), six (6) hours.

(12) Producer shall require the teacher to prepare a written report for each minor covering attendance, grades, etc. These reports shall be given to the minor's parents or guardian to deliver to the minor's regular school at the end of each assignment or at such intervals as required by such school.

E. Supervision

(1) On days when the minor's regular school is in session, Producer must require the minor to report to the teacher immediately upon arrival at the place of employment. When school is in session, the teacher has primary responsibility for the education and supervision of the minor.

(2) Presence of the teacher does not relieve parents, however, of the responsibility of caring for their own children. A parent or guardian must be present at all times while a minor is working, and shall have the right, subject to filming requirements, to be within sight and sound of the minor, except as restricted herein by subsection D.(10).

(3) When a parent is working at the minor's place of employment but not at the scene of employment, either the other parent or a guardian must be present with the minor.

(4) A guardian, as that term is used in this Section, must be at least eighteen (18) years of age, have the written permission of the minor's parent(s) to act as a guardian, and show sufficient maturity to be approved by Producer (and teacher, if teacher is present).

(5) No minor may be sent to wardrobe, make-up, hairdressing, or employed in any manner unless under the general supervision of a teacher, parent or guardian.

(6) If Producer engages any minor under the age of fourteen (14), Producer must designate one (1) individual on each set to coordinate all matters relating to the welfare of the minor and shall notify the minor's parent or guardian and teacher, when one is present, of the name of such individual.

(7) Parents and guardians are not permitted to bring other minors not engaged by Producer to the place of employment without Producer's specific permission.

F. Working Hours

(1) Minors less than six (6) years of age are permitted at the place of employment for six (6) hours (excluding meal periods, but including school time, if any).

(2) Minors who have reached the age of six (6) years but who have not attained the age of nine (9) years may be permitted

at the place of employment for eight (8) hours (excluding meal periods, but including school time).

(3) Minors who have reached the age of nine (9) years but who have not attained the age of sixteen (16) years may be permitted at the place of employment for nine (9) hours (excluding meal periods, but including school time).

(4) Minors who have reached the age of sixteen (16) years but who have not attained the age of eighteen (18) years may be permitted at the place of employment for ten (10) hours (excluding meal periods, but including school time).

(5) The work day for a minor shall begin no earlier than 5:00 a.m. and shall end no later than 10:00 p.m. on evenings preceding school days. On evenings preceding non-school days, the minor's work day shall end no later than 12:30 a.m. on the morning of the non-school day.

(6) If a minor is at location, the minor must leave location as soon as reasonably possible following the end of his or her working day, and may not be held for transportation.

(7) Interviews and fittings for children who are attending school shall be held outside of school hours. Such interviews and fittings shall be held not later than 9:00 p.m. At least two (2) adults shall be present at all times during a fitting.

(8) A minor shall not work more than six (6) consecutive days. However, for this purpose, a day of school only or travel only shall not be counted as one of said consecutive days.

(9) Producer shall set the first call at the beginning of the minor's employment and dismissal on the last day of the minor's employment so as to ensure that the minor will have a twelve (12) hour rest period prior to and at the end of the employment. For example, if a minor's last day of employment is Wednesday, and the minor will be attending school at 8:30 a.m. on Thursday, the minor must be dismissed by 8:30 p.m. on Wednesday.

G. Dressing Rooms

No dressing rooms shall be occupied simultaneously by a minor and an adult performer or by minors of the opposite sex.

H. Play Area

A safe and secure place for minors to rest and play must be provided by Producer.

I. Medical Care and Safety

(1) The minor's parent or guardian must provide Producer a certificate signed by a doctor licensed to practice medicine within the state wherein the minor resides or is employed, stating that the minor has been examined within six (6) months prior to the date he or she was engaged by Producer and has been found to be physically fit.

(2) Prior to a minor's first call, Producer must obtain the written consent of the minor's parent or legal guardian for medical care in the case of an emergency. However, if the parent or legal guardian refuses to provide such consent because of religious convictions, Producer must at least obtain written consent for external emergency aid, provided that the obtaining of such consent is not contrary to the aforementioned religious convictions.

(3) No minor shall be required to work in a situation which places the child in clear and present danger to life or limb. If a minor believes he/she would be in such danger, the parent or guardian may have the teacher and/or stunt coordinator, if either or both are present, discuss the situation with the minor. If the minor persists in his/her belief, regardless of its validity, the minor shall not be required to perform in such situation.

(4) When a minor is asked to perform physical, athletic or acrobatic activity of an extraordinary nature, the minor's parent or guardian shall first be advised of the activity and shall

represent that the minor is fully capable of performing the activity. Producer will comply with reasonable requests for equipment that may be needed for safety reasons.

J. Child Labor Laws

(1) A summary of the applicable state child labor laws governing the employment of the minor shall be kept in the Producer's production office if such summary is readily available.

(2) Any provision of this Section which is inconsistent and less restrictive than any child labor law or regulation in applicable state or other jurisdictions shall be deemed modified to comply with such laws or regulations.

K. Inconsistent Terms

The provisions of this Section shall prevail over any inconsistent and less restrictive terms contained in any other Sections of this Agreement which would otherwise be applicable to the employment of the minor, but such terms shall be ineffective only to the extent of such inconsistency without invalidating the remainder of such Sections.

L. Arbitration

Any dispute between performer and Producer with respect to any provision contained in this Section shall be arbitrable, regardless of the amount of compensation paid or guaranteed to the performer. Any such dispute between the Union and Producers shall likewise be arbitrable. The procedures for such arbitrations shall be those contained in Section 9 hereof.

M. Overnight Location - Expenses

When state law or this Agreement requires that a parent or guardian of a minor be present while such minor is working and such minor is employed on an overnight location under the terms of this Agreement, Producer will, in conjunction with its negotiation for the minor's services, also negotiate in good faith with respect to expenses incurred by the parent or guardian for transportation, lodging and meals that may be required for the assignment and such expenses must be approved in advance. In the case of air transportation, Producer will endeavor to provide for the parent or guardian the same class of transportation, on the same flight as the minor, if reasonably available. In the case of lodging, Producer shall endeavor to provide a room for the parent or guardian in the same facility and adjacent to the minor's room, if reasonably available, provided that a minor under eleven (11) years old may be required to share his/her room with his/her parent or guardian, and a minor eleven (11) years to sixteen (16) years old may be required to share his/her room with a parent of the same sex.

N. Time Cards

On production time reports or time cards submitted to the Union, Producer shall designate minors with a "K" next to the minor's name.

VI. **GLOSSARY OF TERMS FOR YOUNG PERFORMERS**
Common industry terms your child will encounter along the road to his or her career in entertainment. (As seen at http://www.sagaftra.org/content/young-performers-glossary)

YOUNG PERFORMERS GLOSSARY

TERMS

Action: The cue that is shouted when the camera starts rolling

A.D.: Assistant Director

Ad Lib: Made up dialogue that is not scripted; a form of improvisation

Art Director: Person who creates and designs sets

Avail: A courtesy situation extended by an agent to a producer indicating that a performer is available to work a certain job. Avails have no legal or contractual status

Background Talent: Also known as extras

Best Boy: In films, the assistant to the electrician

Billing: The order of the names in the titles or opening credits of a film or television show

Bio (or biography): A résumé in narrative form usually for a printed program or press release

Blocking: The physical movements used by actors in a scene

Booking: A firm commitment to a performer to do a specific job

Boom: An overhead microphone, often used on-set, usually mounted on an extended pole

Breakdown: A detailed listing and description of roles available for casting in a production

Buyout: An offer of full payment in lieu of residuals, when the contract permits

Callback: A follow-up audition

Call sheet: Production term for daily listing of shooting schedule, scenes and cast involved

Call time: The time you are due on a set

Cattle call: Often known as an "open call," a large open audition

Close-up (CU): Camera term for a tight shot of the shoulders and face

Cold reading: An unrehearsed reading of a scene, usually at auditions

Commissions: Percentage of a performer's earnings paid to an agent's managers for their services

Composite: A one-sheet of photos representing an actor's different "looks"

Conflict: Status of being paid for services in a commercial for one advertiser, thereby contractually preventing performing services in a commercial for a competitor

Copy: The script for a commercial or voice-over

Craft services: On-set catering

Dailies: Screening of footage before it is edited

Day-player: A performer hired on a day-to-day basis, rather than under a long term contract

Downgrade: Reduction of a performer's on-camera role from principal to extra

D.P.: Director of Photography; Cinematographer

Dress the set: To add items/props to the set

Drive-on pass: A pass to drive on and park at a studio

Emancipated minor: A minor under 18 who has been given the status of a legal adult by a judge

Employer of Record (EOR): The company responsible for employment taxes and unemployment benefits

Executive Producer: The person responsible for funding a production

EXT. (Exterior): A scene shot outside

Field rep: SAG staff member who ensures contractual compliance on a set

Forced call: A call to work less than 12 hours after dismissal of the previous day

FX (Effects): Special Effects

Gaffer: A crew member who places lighting instruments

GED: General Equivalency Diploma

Gofer: An errand runner

Golden time: Overtime after the 16th hour

Grip: A crew member who moves set pieces or props

Hiatus: Time when a TV series is in between production

Hold: A contractual obligation for a performer to be available for work

Holding fee: Set payment by an advertiser to retain the right to use a performer's services, images or likeness on an exclusive basis

Industrial: Non-broadcast, often educational films

INT. (Interior): A scene shot indoors

In time: The actual call time or start time; also refers to return time from a break

Looping: An in-studio technique matching voice to picture (Also known as ADR)

Meal Penalty: A set fee paid by the producer for failure to provide meals as set by the contract

Monologue: A solo performance by an actor

Out time: The actual time after which you have changed out of wardrobe and are released

Overtime (OT): Work extending beyond the contractual workday

P.A.: Production Assistant

Pan: A camera shot which sweeps from side to side

Pick-up: An added take because of a problem with a shot

Pilot: The first show introducing the characters and situations for a potential series

Popping: A vocal term used to describe the sudden release of blocked air into a microphone causing a popping sound

POV shot: A point of view shot; camera angle from the perspective of one actor

Principal: A performer with lines or special business which advances the storyline

Producer (or Line Producer): The person responsible for the day-to-day decision making on a production

Re-write: Changes in the scripts; often made using color-coded pages

Scale: Minimum payment for services under Union contracts

Scale+ 10: Minimum payment plus 10 percent to cover agent's commission

Script Supervisor: The crew member assigned to record all changes or actions as the production proceeds

Sides: Pages or scenes from a script used for auditions

Sight-and-sound: Parent's right under Union contracts to be within the sight of the child performer at all times

Signatory: An employer who has agreed to produce under the terms of a union contract

Slate: A small chalkboard and clapper device, used to mark and identify shots for editing; also the verbal identification by a performer in a taped audition (i.e. "Slate your name.")

Stage Manager: The person who oversees the technical aspects of an in-studio production

Station 12: At SAG, the office responsible for clearing SAG members to work

Studio Teacher: Set teacher or tutor, hired to provide education to working with young performers; also responsible for enforcing Child Labor Law

Stunt Coordinator: The persons in charge of designing and supervising the performance of stunts and hazardous activities

Submission: An agent's suggestion to a casting director for a role in a certain production

Taft-Hartley: A federal statute which allows 30 days after first employment before being required to join a Union

Take: The clapboard indication of a shot "taken" or printed

Take 5: The announcement of a periodic five minute break

Waivers: Board-approved permission for deviation from the terms of a contract

Walk-on: A very brief role

Wardrobe: The clothing a performer wears on camera

Work Permit: A legal document required to allow a child to work, issued by various state or local agencies

Wrap: finishing a production

VII. CHILD WORK PERMIT INFORMATION (BY STATE)

States Requiring Special Work Permits

- **California**: http://www.dir.ca.gov/dlse/DLSE-CL.htm

- **New York**: http://www.labor.state.ny.us/workerprotection/laborstandards/secure/child_index.shtm

- **New Jersey**: http://lwd.dol.state.nj.us/labor/wagehour/content/child_labor.html

- **New Mexico**: http://www.dws.state.nm.us/careersolutions/CSS-WorkP.html

- **Louisiana**: http://www.laworks.net/Downloads/ORS/MinorIntentionToEmployForm.pdf

State Requirements

- **Alabama**: http://www.alalabor.state.al.us/CD/Movie%20Release.pdf http://www.alalabor.state.al.us/PDFs/Work_Permit_Application.pdf

- **Alaska**: http://labor.state.ak.us/lss/childlaw.htm http://labor.state.ak.us/lss/lssforms.htm

- **Arizona**: http://www.azcommerce.com/Film/Child+Labor+Laws+(Arizona+Youth+Labor+Law).htm

- **Arkansas**: http://www.ark.org/labor/divisions/standards_childlabor.html

- **Colorado**: http://www.colorado.gov/cs/Satellite/CDLE-EmployTrain/CDLE/1248095317847

- **Connecticut**: http://www.ctdol.state.ct.us/wgwkstnd/faqs-minors.htm

- **Delaware**: http://www.delawareworks.com/industrialaffairs/services/LaborLawEnforcementInfo.shtml

- **Florida**: http://www.myfloridalicense.com/dbpr/reg/childlabor/index.html

- **Georgia**: http://www.dol.state.ga.us/em/child_labor.htm

- **Hawaii**: http://www.hawaiifilmoffice.com/film-permitting/filming-regulations/child-labor-law

- **Idaho**: http://labor.idaho.gov/dnn/idl/LaborLaws/tabid/667/Default.aspx

- **Illinois**: http://www.ilga.gov/commission/jcar/admincode/056/05600250sections.html

- **Indiana**: http://www.in.gov/dol/childlabor.htm

- **Kentucky**: http://www.oet.ky.gov/des/pubs/jobser/childlabor. pdf http://labor.ky.gov/dows/doesam/kcll/pages/child-labor-law.aspx

- **Maine**: http://www.maine.gov/labor/labor_laws/wagehour.html

- **Maryland**: http://dllr.maryland.gov/labor/mosh/teenworkers-guide.shtml

- **Massachusetts**: http://www.mass.gov/?pageID=mg2subtopic &L=4&L0=Home&L1=Business&L2=Workplace+%26+Empl oyees&L3=Child+labor+%26+apprenticeships&sid=massgov2

- **Michigan**: http://www.michigan.gov/documents/Work_Per-mit_FACT_SHEET_July_2006_169123_7.pdf

- **Minnesota**: http://www.dli.mn.gov/LS/ChildLabor.asp

- **Mississippi**: http://www.mdes.ms.gov/wps/portal#null

- **Missouri**: http://labor.mo.gov/DLS/YouthEmployment/

- **Montana**: http://erd.dli.mt.gov/labor-standards/child-labor-law/103-montanas-child-labor-law-reference-guide.html http://erd.dli.mt.gov/labor-standards/child-labor-law.html

- **Nevada**: http://www.leg.state.nv.us/NRS/NRS-609.html

- **New Hampshire**: http://www.labor.state.nh.us/youth_employ-ment.asp

- **North Carolina**: http://docsouth.unc.edu/nc/rules1933/rules1933.html

- **Oklahoma**: http://www.ok.gov/odol/Workforce_Protection/Child_Labor/

- **Oregon**: http://www.boli.state.or.us/BOLI/WHD/CLU/index. shtml

- **Pennsylvania**: http://www.dli.state.pa.us/landi/CWP/view. asp?a=185&Q=58124

- **Rhode Island**: http://www.dlt.ri.gov/ls/childlabor.htm

- **South Carolina**: http://www.llr.state.sc.us/Labor/wages/index. asp?file=childlabor.htm

- **South Dakota**: http://dlr.sd.gov/lmic/lb/lbartapr07_youth_ labor_laws.pdf

- **Tennessee**: http://www.state.tn.us/labor-wfd/childlab.html

- **Texas**: http://www.twc.state.tx.us/ui/lablaw/cllsum.html

- **Utah**: http://www.laborcommission.utah.gov/FAQ.html#Minors

- **Vermont**: http://www.labor.vermont.gov/

- **Virginia**: http://www.doli.virginia.gov/laborlaw/laborlaw_ faqs_childlaborlawp1.html http://www.doli.virginia.gov/labor- law/laborlaw_childworkpermits1.html

- **Washington State**: http://www.lni.wa.gov/WorkplaceRights/ TeenWorkers/default.asp

- **Wisconsin**: http://www.dwd.state.wi.us/er/labor_standards_ bureau/child_labor_laws.htm

VIII. SAMPLE TALENT AGREEMENT

[PRODUCTION COMPANY]
[ADDRESS]

Dated: _____

LENDER:

ARTIST:

Re: <u>Employment Agreement</u>

Gentlepersons:

The following will confirm the agreement between you and us relative to the loanout of the services of Artist as provided herein.

1. You agree to furnish the services of Artist in connection with the actor services set forth in the Main Agreement and Standard Terms and Conditions annexed thereto (hereinafter called the "Employment Agreement"), which are attached hereto and made a part hereof as if fully set forth herein. Your employment shall be subject to all of the terms and conditions set forth in the Employment Agreement.

2. Notwithstanding the fact that the Employment Agreement is drafted in the form of an agreement between the Artist and us, it is understood and agreed that you are supplying Artist's services to us and that we are utilizing said services in accordance with the terms and provisions of said Employment Agreement which are hereby expressly incorporated into this Agreement as though set forth in full. We shall have all of the

rights to Artist's services and the results and proceeds thereof, and all other rights which are granted to us in the Employment Agreement and we will become the owner of the results and proceeds of Artist's services as provided in said Employment Agreement to the same extent as though Artist had executed said Employment Agreement and was our employee for hire.

3. For all of your obligations hereunder and all rights granted by you, we shall pay you the compensation to be paid Artist in the Employment Agreement and subject to the terms and conditions of the Employment Agreement. You agree to pay withholding, employment or other taxes required in connection with Artist's services hereunder, and to indemnify and hold us harmless against the paying of any such withholding and employment taxes. We agree to reimburse you for payment to the applicable union or guild for union health, pension and welfare incurred due to Artist's services hereunder, if any. You shall be solely responsible for securing liability insurance and workman's compensation insurance covering Artist on all services rendered by Artist pursuant to the attached Employment Agreement.

4. You warrant that you have the right to enter into this Agreement and to grant the rights and furnish the services herein set forth. Each of us warrants that there are no agreements preventing the fulfilment of this Agreement, or which shall impair or diminish the value of the rights granted hereunder. You further agree to indemnify and hold us harmless from all damages, including reasonable attorneys' fees, which may be suffered by us by reason of any breach of any warranty made by you hereunder.

5. Your I.R.S. Reporting Number is:

6. You shall have the benefit of all agreements, representations and warranties made by us to Artist in the Employment Agreement; provided, however, that you shall not receive any rights hereunder which are greater than those which Artist would have received if Artist had entered into the Employment Agreement.

If the foregoing is in accordance with your understanding of our agreement, please indicate your acceptance by signing in the space provided below.

Yours very truly,

[PRODUCTION COMPANY]

By: _____

Its: _____

AGREED AND ACCEPTED:

[ARTIST]

By: _____

Its: _____

I have read the foregoing Agreement and agree to render all services and to grant all rights necessary to enable _____. ("Lender") to comply fully with its obligations under said Agreement. I agree to indemnify [PRODUCTION COMPANY] by reason of my failure or the failure of Lender to comply fully with any of my or its obligations, and I will primarily guarantee the obligations, representations, warranties and agreements of Lender. I certify that my services are rendered as an employee for hire of Lender, and I agree to look solely to Lender for payment of compensation for my services and discharge of all other obligations of an employer.

_____
[ARTIST] ("Artist")

This Agreement, made as of [DATE], by and between [PRODUC-
TION COMPANY], [PRODUCTION COMPANY ADDRESS]
("Producer"), and [ARTIST] (the "Artist"), [ARTIST'S ADDRESS],
shall set forth the terms and conditions of the employment by Producer of the services of Artist in and in connection with the proposed
television series consisting of thirty (30) minute episodes tentatively
entitled "[SERIES TITLE]" (the "Series"), currently intended for initial
broadcast in the United States on the [TELEVISION CHANNEL], as
follows:

1. <u>Conditions Precedent</u>. All of Producer's obligations under
   this Agreement are expressly conditioned upon and subject
   to Artist delivering to Producer: (a) executed original copies
   of this Agreement prior to Artist's start of services, including
   Artist's and Artist's parent's completion and execution of the
   "Parental Consent" forms attached hereto as Exhibit A and all
   forms which may be required for court approval of this Agreement; (b) completed and signed documents required by any
   governmental authority (including, without limitation, Form
   I-9, W-4, etc.); (c) any and all documentation required by Producer's payroll company (including, a copy of the Articles of
   Incorporation of Artist's loanout corporation, if applicable);
   and (d) any and all other necessary visa forms and/or other
   documents required by the immigration laws or regulations of
   the United States and/or [FOREIGN COUNTRY]. Artist shall
   be responsible for obtaining any such documentation and all
   costs associated therewith shall be borne by Artist at Artist's
   sole expense.

2. <u>First Cycle</u>.

   (a) Artist shall provide acting services in the role of "[ART-
       IST'S ROLE]" in the Series. Artist acknowledges that the
       character "[ARTIST'S ROLE]" existed prior to the produc-
       tion of the Series, and Artist had no part in the creation
       of such character. Producer agrees that, subject to Artist's
       default, disability, death or an event of force majeure, Artist

shall be engaged to render services on a pay-or-play basis for twenty (20) episodes of the Series (the "Guaranteed Episodes"). Producer shall have an exclusive and irrevocable option, exercisable at any time on or before the date which is sixty (60) days following the completion of principal photography of the last Guaranteed Episode, to engage Artist to perform services in connection with up to twenty (20) additional episodes (the "Additional First Cycle Episodes", and collectively with the Guaranteed Episodes, the "First Cycle Episodes"). Artist's engagement hereunder shall commence on a date and at a location reasonably designated by the Producer, and shall continue until the completion of Artist's services in connection with the Guaranteed Episodes.

(b) Artist shall render all services customarily rendered by actors in first-class cable television programs in the United States in connection with the Series including, without limitation, services for lead-ins and lead-outs (whether to commercials or program material), station breaks, narration and related services in connection with the Series, rehearsals, principal photography (including, without limitation, singing and dancing), services for looping, post-synching, retakes, added scenes, taping on-air promotional spots for the Series, and other pre- and post-production activities. All such services shall be subject to the direction and control of Producer including, without limitation, in respect of all financial matters and matters of artistic taste and judgment. Artist shall render services hereunder on such date(s) and at such location(s) as shall be reasonably designated by Producer. It is currently anticipated that Artist's services for principal photography for the Guaranteed Episodes shall commence on a date designated by Producer in or about [DATE] and shall continue thereafter until completion of all services required of Artist in connection with the Guaranteed Episodes, currently anticipated to be [DATE]. Notwithstanding the foregoing, Artist's services shall be required to be on location for approximately two (2) weeks, as reasonably designated by Producer, prior to the commencement of taping for prepro-duction services, including, without limitation, rehearsals, wardrobe, etc.

3. Additional Series Cycle.

(a) Producer shall have an exclusive and irrevocable option (the "Series Option") to engage Artist's services on an additional cycle of Series episodes as Producer shall, from time to time, reasonably designate in its sole discretion (the "Second Cycle"). The Series Option is exercisable on or before the date which is thirty (30) days following Producer's receipt and acceptance of written confirmation from the network or broadcaster of an order for additional episodes of the Series, but in no event later than the date which is twelve (12) months following the delivery to, and acceptance by the broadcaster of the Series of the last episode of the Guaran-teed Episodes (the "Exercise Date").

(b) If Producer exercises the Series Option, Artist shall render services in connection with those episodes of the Series pro-duced for the Second Cycle (the "Second Cycle Episodes") as Producer shall from time to time designate; such services shall commence on such date(s) and be rendered at such location(s) as may be reasonably designated by Producer.

4. Series Compensation.

(a) For the Guaranteed Episodes, the Additional First Cycle Episodes and for each episode in the Second Cycle in which Artist appears (excluding title sequences and episodic recaps), subject to Artist's complete performance of the terms and conditions herein, Producer shall pay to Artist the following episodic rate (the "Episodic Rate") as full com-pensation for Artist's services in connection with the Series and all rights granted therein:

Cycle	Episodic Rate (in U.S. Dollars)
(i) Guaranteed Episodes and Additional First Cycle Episodes	$_____
(ii) Second Cycle	$_____

(b) The Episodic Rate shall be payable on Producer's regular payday the week following the completion of principal photography of each applicable episode; provided that Producer shall pay to Artist, promptly upon Artist's arrival in [LOCATION], an advance of _____ Dollars ($_____), which sum may be deducted and recouped from all sums otherwise payable to Artist hereunder.

(c) The foregoing Episodic Rates are for episodes of up to thirty (30) minutes in length. The compensation payable for any episodes which are greater or lesser in length shall be pro-rated and any such episodes shall be credited proportionately against the number of Guaranteed Episodes; e.g., if a sixty (60) minute Series episode is produced hereafter, it shall constitute two (2) thirty (30) minute episodes for purposes of computing the number of Guaranteed Episodes and Artist shall be entitled to compensation therefor at twice the then applicable Episodic Rate.

(d) In addition to the sums set forth above, for each complete week during which Artist is reasonably required by Producer to be in [OUT OF U.S. LOCATION], Artist shall receive an additional sum of _____ Dollars ($____) as reimbursement for expenses incurred by Artist.

(e) If Producer shall require Artist to take singing and/or dancing lessons, Artist shall do so, provided Producer shall be responsible for the costs thereof.

(f) Artist shall not be entitled to any additional compensation for Artist's services hereunder and/or for the use, reuse or other exploitation of any episodes of the Series, and/or the results and proceeds of Artist's services hereunder, in any media, now known or hereafter developed, except as otherwise set forth in this paragraph and in paragraph 5 below.

(g) Producer may withhold from sums payable to Artist hereunder any amounts it is required to withhold pursuant to applicable federal, state or local law (including, without limitation, the tax laws of [FOREIGN COUNTRY]). No such withholding shall excuse Artist's obligations hereunder (including, without limitation, Artist's obligation to render services hereunder).

5. <u>Additional Services for the Series</u>.

(a) Producer shall have the option to engage Artist's services as an on-camera and/or off-camera performer in connection with the production, manufacturing and distribution of home video devices (e.g., VHS, DVD) embodying episodes of the Series. Such services may include, but will not necessarily be limited to, performing in wrap-around inserts and attending photo shoot sessions for home video packaging.

(b) Producer shall have the option to engage Artist to render services as a performer in connection with audio recording projects (excluding soundtrack albums) during the period when Artist is providing services on the Series.

(c) Producer shall have the option to engage Artist's services as a performer in connection with projects produced for the interactive or multi-media markets (or similar technologies now known or hereafter developed) during the period when Artist is providing services on the Series.

(d) Artist shall receive an amount equal to _____ Dollars ($____) per day for any of the services provided to Producer in connection with paragraphs 5(a), (b) and (c) above.

6. <u>Credit</u>. Subject to network and broadcaster approval, and provided Artist renders material services in a Series episode and appears recognizably in such episode as exhibited, and further

provided Artist is not in material breach hereof, Artist shall receive credit on-screen on all positive prints of each applicable episode of the Series, in no less than third position. All other aspects of credit shall be at Producer's sole discretion. No casual or inadvertent failure by Producer to provide such credit shall be deemed a breach hereof. In the event of a failure to provide such credit, Artist's rights, if any, shall be limited to the right to seek damages in an action-at-law and in no event shall Artist be entitled to seek or obtain injunctive or other forms of equitable relief. Producer shall use reasonable efforts to cure any failure to give Artist credit on a prospective basis, following receipt by Producer of written notice from Artist of such failure. Upon Artist's written request, Producer shall use reasonable efforts to notify Producer's licensees of the credit information hereunder.

7. Travel/Accommodations/Additional Perquisites.

(a) Artist shall be provided with or, at Producer's election, be reimbursed for (a) one (1) round trip business class air transportation (if available and if used) for each of Artist and Artist's parent or legal guardian to and from [LOCA-TION], (b) one (1) two (2) bedroom apartment for use by Artist and Artist's parent or legal guardian during Artist's services in [LOCATION] (including a television, VCR and a telephone for Artist's use and a DSL internet connection, provided that Artist shall be responsible for all telephone calls and any incremental internet charges in excess of the basic access fee), which apartment shall also provide an interior parking space for one (1) car, (c) a one (1) time all-inclusive, non-accountable moving and relocation payment of _____ Dollars (US$_____), (d) ground transportation to and from airports for each of Artist and Artist's parent or legal guardian, (e) subject to the production schedule for the Series, two (2) additional round trip coach class air transportation tickets (if available and if used) for Artist's family member(s) between [HOME] and [LOCATION] for use during Easter vacation, and (f) four (4) additional round trip coach class air transportation tickets (if available and if used) for Artist's family members to and from [LOCATION] for use during the term of Artist's services in [LOCATION]. If Producer exercises the Series Option, Artist shall be provided with or, at Producer's election, be reimbursed for the travel and/or accommodations set forth in paragraph 7(a), (b), (d) and (e) above in connection with such services.

(b) During the term of Artist's services in [LOCATION], Producer shall provide a tutor for Artist.

(c) Producer shall provide to Artist's parent or guardian (provided he/she has a valid driver's license accepted in [LOCATION] and is insurable) with a rental car for his/her personal use (no less than a mid-size sedan with automatic transmission, air conditioning and other standard amenities), during the term of Artist's services in [LOCATION], and Producer shall obtain automobile insurance covering such rental car.

(d) Producer shall provide Artist and Artist's parent or legal guardian with basic health insurance during the term of Artist's services in [LOCATION] hereunder, as available. (The foregoing obligation shall be deemed satisfied by the health insurance provided by the government of [LOCATION] once residency or other like criteria are satisfied.)

(e) Producer shall provide singing and/or dancing lessons for Artist as may be required in connection with Artist's services hereunder, to be determined by Producer in consultation with Artist, which lessons, if any, shall be at Producer's expense.

(f) Producer shall provide a private dressing area to Artist during principal photography of the Series, with a television, couch, internet access and study space, provided that such dressing room shall be no less favorable than the dressing area provided to any other actor in the Series.

8. <u>Work Rules</u>. Producer agrees to abide by work rules for meal periods, rest between days, and rest periods in connection with Artist's services hereunder in a manner consistent with such terms as promulgated in the American Federation of Television and Radio Artists ("AFTRA") National Code of Fair Practice for Network Television Broadcasting (the "Code") as if the Code were applicable hereto and Producer was an AFTRA signatory; provided, however, it is specifically understood that Producer is not a signatory to AFTRA or any other actor's union or guild, and this Agreement is not subject to the terms of said Code or any other collective bargaining agreement.

9. <u>Personal Appearances; Publicity</u>. At Producer's reasonable request, Artist will make a reasonable number of personal appearances and publicity tours in connection with each cycle of episodes hereunder and cooperate fully with Producer and the broadcaster in efforts to promote and publicize the Series, including, without limitation, publicity sessions, personal appearances, interviews and still photography sessions. Artist shall cooperate with producer and the broadcaster with respect to publicity, promotion, affiliate relations and exploitation of the Series, during the term hereof and after the term subject to Artist's reasonable prior contractual commitments. Producer shall arrange for travel and accommodations, if applicable (including coach class air transportation (provided that Producer shall use reasonable efforts to request that [NETWORK], or other applicable distributor, obtain business class air transportation for Artist if available and within budgetary limits) and standard hotel accommodations), at Producer's expense, for Artist and Artist's parent or legal guardian, and Producer shall pay Artist an all-inclusive per diem of _____ Dollars ($_____), in connection with such personal appearances as requested by Producer (but not with respect to any services provided pursuant to paragraph 2(b) above or otherwise during periods of production).

10. <u>Exclusivity</u>. Artist shall be exclusive to Producer in the area of children's and children's-related programming during the term

hereof, including, but not limited to, programming for [OTHER SIMILAR NETWORKS THAT PRODUCE/DISTRIBUTE CONTENT FOR CHILDREN], and shall not perform in a continuing role or as a regular performer (i.e., three (3) or more appearances) on any other episodic or variety television series or perform in any program scheduled for broadcast during the regularly scheduled broadcast time period for the Series. Notwithstanding the foregoing, Artist may appear in a theatrical or made-for-television motion picture during any scheduled production hiatus during the term hereof, provided that Artist provides Producer with written notice promptly upon committing to appear in any such motion picture, and that Artist complies with all other obligations hereunder. Any commitment that Artist makes to render Artist's services for a third party shall be made expressly subject to Artist's obligations to render services for the Series, and Artist shall be available to Producer, to render such Series services on a first-priority, regular, in person, basis at any time during the term hereof. Artist shall not render services to any third party or on Artist's own account which would interfere with Artist's ability to perform Artist's required services for the Series or which may be inconsistent in content, taste and sensibilities with the traditional and family-oriented values of the intended broadcaster of the Series without Producer's prior written approval. If Artist renders services for any third party during the term of this Agreement, Artist's services for the Series shall be rendered on a first priority, regular, in-person basis. The exclusivity provisions hereof shall apply at all times during which Producer has the right to exercise an option for Artist's services hereunder. Artist shall not perform for any third party as any character which Artist created or performed in connection with the Series without the express written consent of Producer, nor may Artist satirize or parody the same or a substantially similar character as that portrayed by Artist in the Series at any time, without Producer's approval, not to be unreasonably withheld. Any television performance by Artist consistent with the foregoing restrictions shall require

Artist to furnish the prospective employer with written notice, with a copy to Producer, regarding time period protection, the production requirements of the Series, and that the premier of any such other television program may not be telecast during the premier of the Series or during the time period the Series is telecast.

11. Court Approval. Artist and Artist's parent hereby authorize Producer or its designees to deduct from any payment to Artist hereunder a reserve in such amount as Producer determines but in no event less than fifteen percent (15%) of Artist's gross earnings or whatever greater or lesser percentage of gross earnings the judge of a court of competent jurisdiction selected by Producer may order deposited in a blocked trust account for the benefit of Artist. Upon Producer's (or Producer's designee's) request, Artist and Artist's parents agree to execute such documents (including, without limitation, the Parental Consent forms, and the Minor's Contract Employment Information Sheet attached hereto as Exhibit A), to participate in such proceedings and otherwise cooperate as Producer shall deem necessary or desirable to obtain an order (in form satisfactory to Producer) signed by a judge of a court of competent jurisdiction (as determined by Producer) approving all of the terms and conditions of this Agreement. Artist and Artist's parents further agree to execute upon Producer's (or Producer's designee's) request documents requesting such court to place the financial aspects of this Agreement under seal. Producer shall afford Artist the right to review and provide Producer with reasonable written comments, at Artist's sole cost and expense, on such further documents within three (3) business days of Artist's receipt thereof (which time period may be reduced due to production, distribution and/or marketing exigencies), and Producer shall give good faith consideration to such written comments, provided that Producer's final determination of form and content of such documents and instruments shall prevail. Upon Artist's written request, Producer shall provide Artist with copies of all final documents.

12. <u>Videocassette</u>. Provided Artist is not in breach or default hereof, Producer shall use good faith efforts to cause [NETWORK], to furnish Artist, upon Artist's written request, with one (1) videocassette and one (1) DVD embodying each episode of the Series in which Artist recognizably appears at such time as such videocassettes and DVDs are made available for purchase by the general public. Artist shall use said DVD and videocassette copy solely for personal, library and reference purposes, and in no event shall such videocassette copy be duplicated or used for any commercial purpose or profit, including, but not limited to, public exhibition.

13. <u>Standard Terms and Conditions</u>. The Standard Terms and Conditions attached hereto are hereby incorporated by reference.

The foregoing, and all attachments hereto, shall constitute the complete and binding agreement of the parties, superseding all prior understandings and communications, express or implied, oral or written, with respect to the subject matter hereof and this Agreement shall not be modified or amended except by a subsequent writing signed by all parties hereto.

ACCEPTED AND AGREED TO: ACCEPTED AND AGREED TO:

[PRODUCER]

By: _____

Its: _____

_____
[ARTIST] ("Artist")

_____
Legal Guardian of Artist

STANDARD TERMS AND CONDITIONS

These Standard Terms and Conditions are incorporated into and made a part of the attached Agreement (the "Main Agreement") dated as of [DATE] by and between [ARTIST] ("Artist") and [PRODUCER] ("Producer") with respect to the services of Artist in and in connection with that proposed one-half (1/2)-hour episodic television series tentatively entitled "[TITLE]" (working title) (the "Series"). References to "this Agreement" or "the Agreement" shall mean the Main Agreement and these Standard Terms and Conditions. In the event of a conflict between any provision of these Standard Terms and Conditions and the Main Agreement in relation to Artist's services, the latter shall prevail. Capitalized terms not defined herein shall have the meaning ascribed to them in the Main Agreement.

1.   Artist's Services. Artist shall render services hereunder commencing on the start date set forth in the Main Agreement and continuing until the completion of all services required by Producer hereunder in connection with the Series. During the period of Artist's services hereunder, Artist's services shall be rendered on an exclusive basis. Artist's services hereunder shall consist of any and all services customarily rendered by actors in the United States television industry in connection with the preproduction, production and postproduction (e.g. looping, dubbing, retakes, added scenes, foreign versions, singing, dancing, trailers and promotional materials, etc.) of the Series and as Producer may require.

2.   Conditions Precedent. This Agreement and Producer's obligations are subject in all respects to the securing of any and all labor permits and visas as may be required by any governmental authority or agency for the purpose of enabling Artist to render services hereunder. Upon Producer's request, Artist shall fully cooperate with Producer in any effort to secure any and all required labor permits and visas. Artist shall be solely responsible for Artist's passport as required.

3.   Performance Standards. Artist hereby warrants and agrees that Artist shall render services hereunder promptly in a diligent, conscientious, artistic and efficient manner to Artist's best abilities, either

alone or in cooperation with others. Artist's services hereunder shall be rendered in such a manner as Producer may direct pursuant to the instructions, suggestions and ideas of and under the control of and at the times and places required by Producer's duly authorized representatives. As between Producer and Artist, Producer shall have all creative and business control with respect to the development, production, distribution and exploitation of the Series.

4. <u>Name and Likeness</u>. Producer shall have the perpetual irrevocable right to use and display Artist's name, approved photograph (subject to the requirements of this Paragraph 4), approved likeness (such approval not to be unreasonably withheld, and to be deemed given if any proposed likeness is not disapproved within three (3) business days after Artist's receipt of a written request therefor, or such shorter period as may be reasonably required by distribution or marketing exigencies), and/or voice and biography (collectively, "Name and/or Likeness") for advertising, publicizing and exploiting the Series, and/or any broadcaster of the Series and/or any results and proceeds of Artist's services, in any and all media throughout the world in perpetuity. Artist shall have a right to approve still photographs intended to be used by Producer, which approval shall not be unreasonably withheld or delayed. Artist shall approve not less than fifty percent (50%) of the still photographs submitted to Artist by Producer for approval, and if Artist does not provide Producer with notice of Artist's selection within three (3) business days (or such shorter time period as may be required due to distribution or marketing exigencies) of receipt of written notice, Producer shall be entitled to select such photographs (i.e., to complete the fifty percent (50%) thereof). Artist grants Producer the irrevocable and exclusive rights, worldwide and in perpetuity, but only in connection with the role portrayed by Artist in the Series, to use and to license the use of Artist's Name and/or Likeness in and in connection with any commercial advertising and publicity tie-ups, merchandising and publishing undertakings. In consideration of such use thereof, Producer shall pay to Artist five percent (5%) of the net receipts actually received by Producer from license fees for such use of Artist's Name and/or Likeness (other than in any listing of credits for the Series or any episode thereof), but if the name and likeness of one

or more other members of the cast of the Series or any other person are licensed in conjunction with Artist's Name and/or Likeness for any such use, the royalty payable to Artist shall be reduced on a pro rata basis to not less than two and one-half percent (2.5%) of such net receipts. Net receipts shall be computed and accounted for in accordance with Producer's customary accounting practices, including deduction of a distribution fee of fifty percent (50%) of gross receipts actually received from agents and distributors, and deduction of all expenses incurred in connection with such merchandising. For purposes of this paragraph 4, posters, soundtrack phonograph records, video devices, and novelizations (including junior novelizations and picture story books) and other publications relating to the Series shall not be deemed undertakings for which any compensation shall be payable under this paragraph. For the avoidance of doubt, if the character of "[CHARACTER]" is depicted without the use of Artist's Name and/or Likeness, no royalty or other payment to Artist shall be required hereunder.

5.   Guilds and Unions. This Agreement and Artist's services shall not be subject to the terms and conditions of any union, guild or collective bargaining agreement(s), unless Producer shall give Artist written notice to the contrary. In the event Producer, in its sole discretion, notifies Artist in writing of a union, guild or collective bargaining agreement which shall govern this Agreement and Artist's services hereunder, the following provisions set forth in this paragraph 5 shall apply:

(a)   Membership. If Producer shall request Artist to do so, then at such time(s) and during such period(s) as it may be lawful for Producer to require, Artist shall become and remain, at Artist's sole cost and expense, a member in good standing of any labor unions or guilds with which Producer may at any time have agreements lawfully requiring such union membership, representing persons performing services of the kind to be performed by Artist hereunder ("Guild Agreement"). Producer shall be entitled to the maximum benefits under such union's collective bargaining agreement and, unless otherwise specified herein, Artist shall be entitled to the minimum benefits under such union's agreements. Without limitation of the foregoing, any fees, residual, reuse or additional compensation which Producer is required to pay to Artist under any Guild Agreement for any exhibition, distribution or other exploitation of the Work, as hereinafter defined (including, without limitation, any television exploitation, supplemental market or other use payments), shall be at the minimum rate required by such applicable Guild Agreement and Producer shall not be required to make any payment other than as required under such applicable agreement.

(b) <u>Superseding Effect of Guild Agreement</u>. Nothing contained in this Agreement shall be construed so as to require the violation of the Guild Agreement, and whenever there is any conflict between any provision of this Agreement and the Guild Agreement, the latter shall prevail. In such event the provisions of this Agreement shall be curtailed and limited only to the extent necessary to permit compliance with the Guild Agreement.

(c) <u>Pension, Health & Welfare & Employer Taxes</u>. Producer agrees to pay on behalf of Artist to any appropriate guild or union having jurisdiction over services performed by Artist hereunder, an amount equal to contributions to pension plans and health and welfare funds required to be under applicable provisions of the Guild Agreement.

(d) <u>No Additional Compensation</u>. All compensation payable to Artist as provided in the Main Agreement shall be in lieu of, and not in addition to, the payments to which Artist may be entitled pursuant to the Guild Agreement.

6. <u>Credit</u>. Producer, in its sole discretion, shall have the right to determine the credit, if any, Artist will receive in connection with the Artist's services hereunder and the form, style, manner and placement and other aspects of such credit. No casual or inadvertent failure by Producer or failure by any third party to accord Artist credit shall be deemed a breach of this Agreement.

7. <u>Ownership</u>. (a) Producer shall own all right, title and interest in and to, and the results and proceeds of Artist's services hereunder, and each element(s) and part(s) thereof (collectively, "Work") in perpetuity in any and all media now known or hereafter devised throughout the world. Without limitation of the foregoing, Artist hereby acknowledges that the Work is specially ordered or commissioned by Producer for use

as a contribution to an audio visual work and that all such Work shall be considered a work made for hire under the United States Copyright Act. Producer shall be considered the sole author thereof for all purposes (including, without limitation, all forms of motion picture, television, digital television, video and computer games, video cassette and video or laser disc, any computer assisted media (including but not limited to CD-ROM, CD-I and similar disc systems, interactive media and multi-media and other devices), character sequel, remake, theme park, stage plays, sound recordings, merchandising and all allied ancillary and subsidiary rights therein) and shall own all of the rights comprised in and to the copyright and renewals and extensions of copyright of such Work and that only Producer shall have the right to copyright the same and that Producer may copyright or renew or extend the copyright to the same in Producer's name or the name of its nominee(s). To the extent that the Work or any element thereof does not vest in Producer as a work made for hire, Artist hereby irrevocably assigns and transfers in whole to Producer all right, title and interest in and to such Work and the results and proceeds thereof, including, without limitation, all copyrights and renewals and extensions of copyright therein throughout the universe, in all languages, in perpetuity, to the extent that Artist has, had or will have any interest therein for exploitation in any and all media now known or hereafter devised throughout the world. The assignment by Artist hereunder also includes, without limitation, the assignment, on Artist's own behalf and on behalf of Artist's heirs, executors, administrators and assigns, in perpetuity, of all rental and lending rights under national laws (whether implemented pursuant to the EC Rental and Lending Rights Directive or otherwise) to which Artist may now be or hereafter become entitled with respect to the Work and Artist acknowledges that the consideration hereunder includes consideration for all such lending and rental rights and is an adequate part of the revenue derived or to be derived from said rights and constitutes equitable remuneration. Without limitation of the foregoing, Artist agrees, on Artist's own behalf and on behalf of Artist's heirs, executors, administrators and assigns, not to institute, support, maintain or permit directly or indirectly any litigation or proceedings instituted or maintained on the ground that Producer's (or its designee's) exercise of the rights granted to Producer in the Work in any way constitutes an infringement or violation of any rental or lending right. For the avoidance of doubt, Producer is not transferring to Artist any right to or interest in any copyright, trademark or service mark relating to any copyright, trademark, service mark or other proprietary property (or to any elements of any of the foregoing) owned or controlled by Producer, or any affiliate or subsidiary thereof.

(b)   To the full extent permitted by applicable law, Artist hereby irrevocably assigns to Producer (or irrevocably waives, in the event assignment is not permissible) any and all benefits of any provision of law known as "droit moral," "moral rights," or any similar law. Without limiting the foregoing, Artist agrees not to institute, support, maintain, or authorize any action or lawsuit based, in whole or in part, on any purported violation of any such law, including without limitation any action or lawsuit brought on the ground that any motion picture, sound recording, or other work produced hereunder in any way constitutes a violation of Artist's moral rights or constitutes a defamation or mutilation of the Work or any part thereof, or contains any unauthorized variation, alteration, modification, change, or translation of the Work.

8.   Warranties and Indemnities. (a) Artist hereby represents and warrants that (i) Artist is not and will not be under any obligation or disability, created by law or otherwise, which in any manner or to any extent prevent or restrict Artist from entering into and freely performing this Agreement or from performing as herein provided, (ii) Artist has the right to enter into and grant the rights granted in this Agreement and to furnish and/or render services as herein provided, and (iii) any and all incidents, dialogue, characters, actions, "gags," material, ideas, inventions and other literary, dramatic and musical material written, composed, submitted, added, improvised, interpolated and invented by Artist pursuant to this Agreement shall be wholly original and shall not infringe upon or violate any copyright of or the right of privacy or any other rights of any person or entity and shall not constitute a libel or slander of any person, firm or corporation. Artist shall indemnify and hold Producer and its officers, agents, employees, representatives and licensees harmless from and against any and all claims,

damages, liabilities, costs and expenses (including, without limitation, attorneys' fees and costs) arising out of any breach or alleged breach by Artist of any warranty, covenant, condition or agreement made or to be performed by Artist under the terms of this Agreement. Producer shall be accorded full control of the defense and/or settlement of any claims, including the right to engage its own counsel.

(b)   Producer hereby represents and warrants that Producer has the right to enter into this Agreement and perform its obligations in connection therewith. Producer will indemnify and hold harmless Artist from and against any and all claims, damages, liabilities, judgments, losses, cost and expenses (including, without limitation, reasonable outside attorneys' fees and costs), suffered or incurred by Artist due to Producer's development, production or exploitation of the Series or due to a breach by Producer of any representation or warranty under this Agreement, except insofar as such claim may be related to a breach by Artist of any of Artist's representations, warranties, covenants and/or agreements hereunder.

9.   Remedies. It is hereby agreed and understood that the services of Artist to be furnished hereunder are extraordinary, unique, and not replaceable, and that there is no fully adequate remedy at law for breach of this Agreement by Artist, and that in the event of such breach by Artist, Producer shall be entitled to equitable relief by way of injunction or otherwise. Artist recognizes and confirms that in the event of a failure or omission by Producer constituting a breach of its obligations under this Agreement, the damage, if any, caused Artist by Producer is not irreparable or sufficient to entitle Artist to injunctive or other equitable relief. Consequently, Artist's rights and remedies shall be limited to the right, if any, to obtain damages at law and Artist shall not have any right in such event to terminate or rescind this Agreement or any of the rights granted to Producer hereunder or to enjoin or restrain the development, production, distribution, exhibition or exploitation of the Series and/or any of the rights granted to Producer pursuant to this Agreement.

10.   No Obligation to Proceed. Nothing in this Agreement shall obligate Producer actually to utilize Artist's services or to exploit the results and proceeds of Artist's services hereunder or to produce or exploit the

Series. Subject to paragraph 11 below, if Producer elects not to utilize Artist's services, payment to Artist for the Guaranteed Episodes at the Episodic Rate therefor (the "Guaranteed Compensation") and any other compensation, if any, earned by Artist prior to Producer discontinuing Artist's services at the times that such amounts would otherwise be payable hereunder constitutes discharge in full of all of Producer's obligations to Artist under this Agreement, provided that Artist will have an obligation to use best efforts to mitigate Producer's payment of such Guaranteed Compensation. If Artist earns any compensation from any third party during the period during which Artist would have rendered services hereunder if Producer had not exercised its pay-or-play right pursuant hereto, such third party compensation will offset such Guaranteed Compensation payable by Producer. In the event Producer pays Artist such Guaranteed Compensation prior to Artist earning any such third party compensation, if and to the extent Artist subsequently earns such third party compensation, at Producer's election, Artist will reimburse Producer and/or Producer will be entitled to deduct from any and all amounts subsequently payable to Artist hereunder pursuant to any applicable other agreement between Producer and Artist for Artist's services, an amount equal to such third party compensation but not to exceed the amount of such Guaranteed Compensation previously paid Artist by Producer.

11. <u>Default, Disability and Force Majeure</u>. (a) Producer shall have the right at its sole election to suspend, extend and/or terminate this Agreement following any one or more events of Artist's breach, default, disability, death or any so-called "force majeure." Artist shall not be entitled to any compensation during any suspension. Artist shall have the one time right to cure any non-material breach or default within twenty-four (24) hours of written notice thereof, which time may be reduced due to production, distribution and/or marketing exigencies. For the avoidance of doubt, a breach pursuant to paragraph 11(b) below shall be deemed a material breach. Producer shall not suspend Artist's services hereunder for an event of force majeure, unless all other third-party personnel (i.e., not employees of Producer) engaged to render services on the Series are similarly suspended or terminated, as the case may be. If a suspension due to a force majeure event continues for more

than twelve (12) consecutive weeks, Artist shall have the right, upon written notice to Producer, to terminate this Agreement, provided that if within five (5) business days after Producer's receipt of Artist's written notice, Producer terminates the suspension by written notice to Artist, then Artist's termination shall be void, Artist's services and the running of time hereunder shall resume, and Producer shall have no further right to suspend or terminate by reason of the event of force majeure upon which the suspension was based.

(b)   If at any time Artist should do any act or thing which shall be an offense involving moral turpitude or commit any criminal offense, become involved in any situation or occurrence which degrades Artist in society or brings Artist into public disrepute, contempt, scandal or ridicule or which insults the community or any substantial group thereof, or which reflects unfavorably upon Artist, Producer, an exhibitor of the Series or the sponsor or sponsors, or its or their advertising agencies, if any, or if Artist has previously engaged in such behavior without Producer's knowledge but information in regard thereto should become public, Producer may, at Producer's election, deem Artist as having materially breached this Agreement and Producer may terminate or suspend Artist's engagement as set forth hereunder.

(c)   In the event this Agreement is terminated pursuant to this paragraph 11, Producer shall be released and discharged from any liability or obligation whatsoever to Artist hereunder, including the obligation to pay any compensation whatsoever to Artist. Payment of any compensation accrued and unpaid prior to the termination shall be subject to all of Producer's rights and remedies against Artist (including the right of offset) for Artist's default.

(d)   Neither the expiration nor termination of this Agreement, or of Artist's services hereunder, shall diminish, impair, modify or otherwise affect any of the provisions hereof capable of surviving such expiration or termination, including, without limitation, provisions respecting Producer's ownership of the Series and all elements thereof, the grant of rights to Producer in and to the results and proceeds of Artist's services hereunder, representations and warranties, indemnification, Artist's waiver of injunctive relief, and construction.

(e) Artist agrees that if Artist is suspended by reason of default or disability and during this period of suspension the Producer produces episodes of the Series, then the number of Guaranteed Episodes, if any, shall be reduced by one (1) for each episode so produced by the Producer.

(f) Artist agrees that if by reason of a force majeure, the broadcaster reduces the number of episodes ordered for the then applicable Cycle, the number of Guaranteed Episodes, if any, shall be reduced by one (1) for each episode so reduced by the broadcaster.

12. <u>Workers' Compensation</u>. In the event that Artist's services are being furnished to Producer through a loanout company (the "Lender"), then notwithstanding that Lender is furnishing services to Producer, and solely for the purpose of any and all applicable Workers' Compensation statutes, an employment relationship shall be deemed to exist between Artist and Producer such that Producer is Artist's special employer and Lender is Artist's general employer (as the terms "special employer" and "general employer" are understood for purposes of Workers' Compensation statutes). The rights and remedies, if any, of Artist and Artist's heirs, executors, administrators, successors and assigns against Producer and/or Producer's officers, directors, agents, employees, successors, assigns or licensees, by reason of injury, illness, disability or death arising out of or occurring in the course of Artist's rendition of services hereunder shall be governed by and limited to those provided under such Workers' Compensation statutes, and neither Producer, nor Producer's officers, directors, agents, employees, successors, assigns or licensees, shall have any other obligation or liability by reason of any such injury, illness, disability or death. If the applicability of any Workers' Compensation statutes to the engagement of Artist's services hereunder is dependent upon or affected by, an election on the part of Lender or Artist, such election is hereby made by Lender and/or Artist in favor of such application, it being expressly agreed that such remedies and liabilities afforded Producer are not less and no greater than had Artist been employed by Producer directly.

13. <u>Assignment and Lending</u>. This Agreement is non-assignable by Artist. This Agreement shall inure to the benefit of Producer's

successors, assignees, licensees and grantees and associated, affiliated and subsidiary companies and Producer and any subsequent assignee may freely assign this Agreement, in whole or in part, to any party provided that such party assumes and agrees in writing to keep and perform all of the executory obligations of Producer hereunder.

14. <u>FCC Obligations</u>. Artist acknowledges that Artist is familiar with the applicable provisions of the Federal Communications Act, as amended, respecting disclosure of payments to individuals connected with broadcasts, and the rules and regulations of the Federal Communications Commission, and Artist agrees to comply with same. Artist's compliance with the foregoing shall be of the essence of this Agreement.

15. <u>No Waiver</u>. No waiver by Producer of any breach or default hereunder shall be deemed to be a waiver of any preceding or subsequent breach or default.

16. <u>Notices</u>. All notices which either party may wish to serve and may be required to serve on the other hereunder shall be in writing, and may be served by personal delivery thereof, or by certified or registered mail, return receipt requested, addressed to the respective parties at their addresses hereinabove set forth, with copies of notices to Producer to: [ATTORNEY'S ADDRESS]. Notices shall be deemed given on the date of personal delivery, the date of mailing, or the date of delivery to the overnight express service with all charges prepaid. Either party hereto may from time to time designate in writing a different address for such service.

17. <u>Insurance</u>. Producer may obtain at its sole expense, accident or other customary insurance on Artist, and Artist agrees to furnish information, to fill out forms, and to undergo medical examinations by physicians retained by Producer, as required. The proceeds of any insurance shall be solely Producer's. If any such examination establishes a substantial doubt as to Artist's physical ability to complete Artist's services hereunder, Producer may terminate this Agreement. If Artist shall fail or be unable to qualify for such insurance without restrictions and at the usual premium, Producer shall have the right to terminate this Agreement. Producer may also require Artist to undergo physical examination by physicians selected

by Producer to determine if Artist is or may become incapacitated. Artist may have a physician selected by Artist present at any physical examination, at Artist's expense.

18. <u>Further Instruments</u>. Artist shall promptly execute, acknowledge and deliver to Producer, or promptly procure the execution, acknowledgment and delivery to Producer, of any and all further agreements and instruments which Producer may deem necessary or expedient to effectuate the purposes of this Agreement.

19. <u>Publicity Restriction</u>. Neither Artist nor Artist's representatives may, individually or jointly, or by means of press agents or publicity or advertising agencies, employed or paid by Artist otherwise, circulate, publish, or otherwise disseminate any news stories or articles, books, trade ads, or other publicity, containing Artist's name and relating directly or indirectly to Artist's employment, the subject matter of this Agreement, the Series or the services to be rendered by Artist or others in connection with the Series unless the same are first approved by Producer, in Producer's sole discretion.

20. <u>Outside Activities</u>. (a) Artist agrees not to engage in any activity which, in Producer's opinion, will subject Artist to undue risk of injury or death, including, but not limited to, the racing of cars, motorcycles, boats, planes, and other vehicles, operation of a motorcycle at any time without the proper use of a helmet, flying in private planes, skydiving, driving under the influence of alcohol or drugs, use of controlled substances, etc.

(b) Artist is aware and agrees that a material inducement for and a condition of Artist's engagement hereunder has been and shall continue to be Artist's physical appearance and that any change(s) or alteration(s) thereto may have an impact upon Producer's business, production activities and/or creative expression. In connection therewith, Artist agrees to consult with and obtain the written approval of Producer before changing or altering Artist's physical appearance in any manner (e.g., hair length, style or color, facial characteristics, weight, etc.). Any change or alteration in Artist's physical appearance not pre-approved by Producer in writing shall constitute a material breach by Artist, entitling Producer in its sole discretion and without limitation to any and all other rights and remedies it may have, to terminate this Agreement or to suspend and/or extend this Agreement during the period of such changed or altered appearance as if such changed or altered appearance were an event of force majeure. In the event that permission is granted by Producer for Artist to alter Artist's physical appearance in connection with a role outside of the Series during a hiatus period, Artist shall return Artist's physical appearance to that last seen in connection with the Series no later than start of pre-production services for the next Cycle.

21.   Confidentiality. Artist agrees that any information Artist learns during the course of or in connection with Artist's engagement hereunder concerning Producer's (and/or any financier(s) and/or exhibitor(s) of the Series) business operations, strategies, future plans, financial affairs, or any other information concerning Producer (and/or such financier(s) and/or exhibitor(s)), their parent, subsidiary and/or affiliated companies, is confidential and proprietary, and Artist will not disclose any such information to any third party.

22.   Drafting History. In resolving any dispute or construing any provision hereunder, there shall be no presumptions made or inferences drawn because the attorneys for one of the parties drafted the Agreement, because of the drafting history of the Agreement, or because of the inclusion of a provision not contained in a prior draft or the deletion of a provision contained in a prior draft.

23.   Legal Counsel. Artist acknowledges that Artist has been advised to obtain, and have obtained, legal counsel to provide Artist with independent advice as to the contents of this Agreement. Artist further acknowledges that this Agreement has been made freely and voluntarily and that Artist is signing same with full knowledge and understanding of all of its terms.

24.   Miscellaneous. This Agreement shall be construed in accordance with the laws of the State of [STATE] (including the applicable Statute of Limitations) applicable to agreements executed and wholly performed within such state. If any term or provision of this

Agreement or the application thereof to any party or circumstance shall, to any extent, be invalid and/or unenforceable, the remainder of this Agreement and the application of such term or provision to any other party(ies) or circumstance(s) other than those to which it is held invalid and/or unenforceable, shall not be affected thereby, and each such other term and provision of this Agreement shall be valid and be enforceable to the fullest extent permitted by law. Nothing herein contained shall be deemed to constitute a partnership between or joint venture by the parties hereto, nor shall either party be deemed the agent of the other. Neither party shall hold itself out contrary to this paragraph. Neither party shall become liable for any representation, act or omission of the other contrary to the provisions hereof. All remedies accorded herein or otherwise available to either Producer or Artist shall be cumulative, and no one such remedy shall be exclusive of any other. This Agreement constitutes the entire agreement and supersedes all prior oral and written agreements and understandings between the parties hereto with respect to the subject matter hereof. Neither Producer nor Artist have made any representation, warranty, covenant or undertaking of any nature whatsoever, express or implied, in connection with or relating to this Agreement other than as herein expressly set forth.

Exhibit A

PARENTAL AGREEMENT

THIS PARENTAL AGREEMENT is made and entered into as of [DATE], by and among [PRODUCER], [PRODUCER'S ADDRESS] (hereinafter referred to as "Producer") and [ARTIST] [ARTIST'S ADDRESS] (hereinafter referred to as "Artist") and [PARENT] ("Parent").

WITNESSETH

WHEREAS, Producer is engaging Artist, pursuant to the actor's agreement dated as of [DATE], including the standard terms and conditions annexed thereto (sometimes referred to as the "Contract" [and as hereinafter more fully defined]), to render performing services in connection with the proposed television series tentatively entitled "[TITLE]" (hereinafter referred to as the "Series");

WHEREAS, Parent is the natural Parent of Artist and has sole legal custody and care of the Artist; and

WHEREAS, the parties hereto contemplate and understand that Producer may file a petition in a court of competent jurisdiction in the state of [STATE], [STATE] or [FOREIGN COUNTRY] (hereinafter sometimes referred to as the "Court") seeking judicial approval by such court of the Contract;

NOW, THEREFORE, as additional consideration for Producer's entering into the Contract, Producer considering using the results and proceeds of Artist's services in the Series and in ancillary and subsidiary rights relating to the Series pursuant to the Contract and for other good and valuable consideration, the parties hereto do hereby agree as follows:

1.   Parent represents, warrants and agrees that the recitals hereinabove set forth are true and correct, that no judgment, order or decree has been made by any court awarding the custody of Artist to any other person or appointing any other person guardian of Artist or Artist's

estate or in any manner affecting the status or the rights of Parent as the parent of Artist, that Artist has not been emancipated, and that Parent has not in any way relinquished (i) the earnings of Artist under the Contract or (ii) the right to collect, receive or control such earnings under the Contract, except as hereinafter expressly provided in paragraph 4.

2. Parent hereby represents, warrants and agrees that during the term of the Contract, Parent will cause Artist to honor Artist's commitments under the Contract, at such place or places as Producer may from time to time direct and to duly observe and perform each and all of the obligations undertaken by Artist pursuant to the Contract, and that Artist will not at any time disaffirm the Contract by reason of Artist's minority, or otherwise.

3. Parent hereby consents and agrees that in the event that Artist fails duly to observe and perform any or all of Artist's obligations under the Contract or Parent fail duly to observe and perform any or all of Parent's obligations hereunder, Parent will indemnify and hold harmless Producer and Producer's successors and assigns from and against all damages, costs, liabilities, expenses, or other losses including, without limitation, reasonable outside attorneys' fees, arising out of each such failure by Artist or Parent.

4. Parent hereby irrevocably and perpetually releases and relinquishes to Artist all salary and compensation payable to Artist pursuant to the Contract, and Parent hereby agrees that she is not entitled to receive or to claim any such salary or compensation or demand that Producer pay such salary or compensation (or any part thereof) to Parent or anyone other than Artist, unless pursuant to instructions from Artist.

5. Parent hereby fully consents to and approves the execution by Artist of the Contract. Parent consents to and approves of Artist's rendering services pursuant to the Contract. Parent hereby acknowledges that Parent has read the Contract and is familiar with all of the terms, covenants and conditions contained therein and is satisfied that the Contract is fair, just and equitable and is for the benefit of Artist. Parent further agrees not to revoke said consent and approvals during the minority of Artist, or thereafter.

6.   Parent hereby agrees that Producer may petition the Court as provided by law, for confirmation and approval of the Contract. Parent further agrees that a copy of this Parental Agreement may be filed with such petitions as evidence of the consent herein granted. Parent agrees that a portion of the sums payable to Artist under the Contract, as the Court shall determine to be proper, may be set aside in a federally insured blocked trust fund or savings account or other similar account (the "Trust") to be held and preserved for Artist, subject to the provisions of the order of the Court or to further an order of the Court. Pending such order of the Court, Parent agrees that the Producer may withhold from sums otherwise payable to Artist pursuant to the Contract an amount reasonably anticipated by Producer to be required by such Court.

7.   Parent hereby fully consents to be named as trustee, guardian or such other similarly entrusted designee of the Trust that the Court may designate for Artist's benefit.

8.   Producer, Artist and Parent hereby agree that Producer may petition the Court, as provided by law, to place under seal any petitions or orders and the copies of the Contract and the Parental Agreement which are filed with the Court for confirmation and approval of the Contract.

9.   This Parental Agreement shall apply to the Contract, to all modifications and extensions thereof and amendments thereto and to any employment agreement between Producer and Artist which may be substituted in full or in part for the Contract.

10.   Parent hereby stipulates and agrees to waive any notice of hearing and hearing required by Section 35.03 of the New York Arts and Cultural Affairs Law or any similar statute in any other jurisdiction with respect to Court approval and confirmation of the Contract.

11.   As used herein, the "Contract" shall mean the actor's agreement including the standard terms and conditions annexed thereto, dated as of [DATE], and any and all documents and agreements as may reasonably be required to further or more formally evidence or effectuate Artist's and/or Producer's rights and/or obligations according to the terms of the actor's agreement, including the standard terms and conditions

annexed thereto, and all amendments, modifications, extensions and substitutions thereof.

12.   This Parental Agreement shall inure to the benefit of and be binding jointly and severally upon the parties hereto, their respective successors, assigns, next of kin, heirs, administrators, executors, officers and agents, as the case may be.

IN WITNESS WHEREOF, the parties hereto have executed this Parental Agreement as of the date hereinabove first set forth.

[PRODUCER]

By: _____

Title: _____

_____

Artist:

_____

Mother:

Bibliography

Beer, Steven C., and Kathryne E. Badura, "The New Renaissance: A Breakthrough Time for Artists," *Berkeley Journal of Entertainment and Sports Law 1* (2012). Available at: http://scholarship.law.berkeley.edu/bjesl/vol1/iss1/5.

Carson, Nancy. *Raising a Star*. St. Martin's Griffin. New York, NY. 2005, p. 195.

Coogan Law. Available at: http://www.sag.org/content/coogan-law. Last visited December 28, 2014.

Department of Industrial Relations: Division of Labor Standards Enforcement (DSLE). Available at: http://www.dir.ca.gov/dlse/DLSE-CL.htm. Last visited December 28, 2014.

Julia Nunes. Available at http://www.facebook.com/#!/junumusic. Last visited December 28, 2014.

New York State Department of Labor. Child Performer: Certificates and Permits. Available at: http://www.labor.state.ny.us/workerprotection/laborstandards/secure/child_index.shtm. Last visited December 28, 2014.

New York State Department of Labor. Child Performer: The Child Performer Education and Trust Act of 2003. Available at: http://www.labor.state.ny.us/workerprotection/laborstandards/secure/childperformer-FAQ.shtm. Last visited December 28, 2014.

NY Arts and Cultural Affairs Law ≤35.03. *See also* California Family Code ≤6750. (Providing precise details on what must be included in a petition for judicial approval of a minor contract).

Screen Actors Guild—Information for Parents of Young Performers: Talking to the SAG Representative on set. Available at http://www.sag.org/content/for-parents. Last visited December 28, 2014.

Spevak, Jeff. Democrat & Chronicle—Young Musicians Find a New Wave of Funding. January 26, 2012. Available at http://roc.democratandchronicle.com/article/20120127/GROUP01/301240005/Teddy%20Geiger,%20Julia%20Nunes,%20Kickstarter,%20PledgeMusic. Last visited December 28, 2014.

Van Patten, Dick, and Peter Berk. *Launching Your Child in Show Biz: A Complete Step-By-Step Guide*. Los Angeles: General Group, 1997.

Young Performers: CBA ≤50: Employment of Minors. Available at: http://www.sagaftra.org/files/sag/2005theatricalagreement.pdf. Last visited December 28, 2014.

Notes

1 Beer, Steven C. and Kathryne E. Badura, "The New Renaissance: A Breakthrough Time For Artists," *Berkeley Journal of Entertainment and Sports Law*, Vol. 1, Issue 1., 2012.

2 Van Patten, Dick, and Peter Berk. *Launching Your Child in Show Biz: A Complete Step-By-Step Guide.* Los Angeles: General Group, 1997.

3 Van Patten, p. 20.

4 Van Patten, pp. 179-80.

5 Department of Industrial Relations: Division of Labor Standards Enforcement (DLSE). Available at: http://www.dir.ca.gov/dlse/DLSE-CL.htm. Last visited December 27, 2014.

6 New York State Department of Labor. Child Performer: Certificates and Permits. Available at: http://www.labor.state.ny.us/workerprotection/laborstandards/secure/child_index.shtm. Last visited December 27, 2014.

7 New York State Department of Labor. Child Performer: The Child Performer Education and Trust Act of 2003. Available at: http://www.labor.state.ny.us/workerprotection/laborstandards/secure/childperformerFAQ.shtm. Last visited December 27, 2014.

8 SAG-AFTRA has also composed a "Young Performers Handbook," available for download on their website at http://youngperformers.sagaftra.org/resources.

9   Young Performers: CBA ≤ 50: Employment of Minors. Available at: http://www.sagaftra.org/files/sag/2005theatricalagreement.pdf. Last visited December 27, 2014.

10   SAG-AFTRA—Information for Parents of Young Performers: Talking to the SAG-AFTRA Representative on Set. http://www.sagaftra. org/content/education-job-one. Last visited December 27, 2014.

11   Children are, however, held to their contracts if they involve necessities such as food, clothing, shelter, etc., but this exception does not come into play in the entertainment contracts discussed here.

12   See NY Arts and Cultural Affairs Law ≤35.03. See also California Family Code ≤6750. (Providing precise details on what must be included in a petition for judicial approval of a minor contract).

13   Van Patten, Dick, Peter Berk, *Launching Your Child in Show Biz: A Complete Step-By-Step Guide,* p. 56.

14   Van Patten, p. 132.

15   Ron notes that there is considerably more competition for girls since they tend to be more interested in pursuing a career in music and entertainment than are boys.

16   Coogan Law. Available at: http://www.sagaftra.org/content/coogan-law-full-text. Last visited November 19, 2013.

17   Consult your attorney or a tax professional to determine, with certainty, what expenses you can and cannot be reimbursed for.

18   Langland, Connie. "For sisters, the stage is the setting for learning The Arcieros' Band is a full-time gig. Home school helps them fit academics and entertaining into their schedule," *Philadelphia Inquirer.* November 14, 2000. Available at http://articles.philly.com/2000-11-14/ news/25614376_1_home-schooling-school-night-local-school.   Last visited December 28, 2014.

19 See http://www.lawny.org/index.php/family-self-help-140/other-family-law-self-help-75/142-emancipation. Last visited December 28, 2014. For a list of other state regulations on emancipation of minors, see http://www.law.cornell.edu/wex/table_emancipation. Last visited December 28, 2014.

20 Pricing. Available at http://www.dittomusic.com/pricing. Last visited December 28, 2014.

21 Ditto Artists. http://www.dittomusic.com/artists. Last visited December 28, 2014.

22 CNN.com - Transcripts. Available at http://edition.cnn.com/TRANSCRIPTS.1009/25/cnr.07.html, last viewed March 22, 2012.

23 Julia Nunes. Available at http://www.facebook.com/#!/junumusic. Last viewed March 23, 2012.

24 Jeff Spevak, Democrat & Chronicle - Young Musicians Find a New Wave of Funding. January 26, 2012. Available at http://roc.democratandchronicle.com/article/20120127/GROUP01/301240005/Teddy%20Geiger,%20Julia%20Nunes,%20Kickstarter,%20PledgeMusic. Last visited December 28, 2014.

25 See http://www.seedandspark.com/. Last visited December 28, 2014.

26 See http://www.imdb.com/name/nm2180154/ (Listing Jessica's acting résumé.) Last visited December 28, 2014.

27 See http://www.peppinamusic.com/. Last visited December 28, 2014. See also http://www.hitrecord.org/users/ppeppina. Last visited December 28, 2014.

28 See http://www.hitrecord.org/. Last visited December 28, 2014.

29 Carson, Nancy. *Raising a Star*. St. Martin's Griffin. New York, 2005, p. 195.

Index

Books from Allworth Press

Allworth Press is an imprint of Skyhorse Publishing, Inc. Selected titles are listed below.

An Actor's Guide: Your First Year in Hollywood
By Michael St. Nicholas and Lisa Mulcahy (paperback, 6 x 9, 316 pages, $19.99)

A Life in Acting: The Actor's Guide to Creative and Career Longevity
by Lisa Mulcahy (paperback, 6 x 9, 192 pages, $16.95)

Actor Training the Laban Way: An Integrated Approach to Voice, Speech, and Movement
by Barbara Adrian (paperback, 7 ⅜ x 9 ¼, 208 pages, $27.95)

Busine
by Ch

Creati
by Gle

The H
by Mc

The L
by Fa

Maste
for B ly
by Jar

Prom
by Gle

Starti
by Jas

Starti
by Ta

Voice
by Jar

VO: 7
by Ha

To see